OPTIONS TRADING STRATEGIES

How To Build A Six-Figure Income With Options Trading Using The Best-proven Strategies For Intermediate and Advanced. The Top Tactics to Know for Beginner and Veteran Options Traders for Successful Gains

Francisco Harris

Disclaimer

All erudition supplied in this book are specified for educational and academic purpose only. The author is not in any way in charge of any outcomes that emerge from utilizing this book. Constructive efforts have been made to render information that is both precise and effective. However, the author is not to be held answerable for the accuracy or use/misuse of this information.

Foreword

I will like to thank you for taking the very first step of trusting me and deciding to purchase/read this life-transforming book. Thanks for investing your time and resources on this product.

I can assure you of precise outcomes if you will diligently follow the specific blueprint I lay bare in the information handbook you are currently checking out. It has transformed lives, and I firmly believe it will equally change your own life too.

All the information I provided in this Do It Yourself piece is easy to absorb and practice.

INTRODUCTION

Options are among the most potent money-making asset classes ever devised. They were not designed as a money-making tool. Instead, their primary purpose for existing is to limit risks associated with the portfolio. Whether you are considering a portfolio of one stock, a hundred stocks, stocks mixed with some commodities, or other related combinations, options can be used to either improve your portfolio's return on capital, take advantage of the opportunity to improve yield, or limit your investment risks by exchanging a little revenue capacity for the "insurance coverage" a long option offers. If you are looking to buy an option with the aim of limiting your risk, somebody has to be on the other side of the trade.

In years past, the opposite of the trade was generally taken by professional options traders. The vocational options trader was a legendary creature who made thousands of dollars every day by "picking the pocket" of the corrupt specific financier. The professional options trader was simply someone who understands the fact that options trading is nothing more than an exercise in basic probability theory. And this possibility theory is easy enough to find out; with a little time and effort, many people can master it and use it for their advantage.

Today options markets are, for the many part, so efficient that you can trade either side of a narrowly estimated market. Thus, there is nobody out there picking anyone's pockets. Options provide the fairest, most equal-opportunity one can expect.

When most investors hear the words options trading, they believe "too much danger," they believe "calculus ...too complex," they think "too time-consuming," and they believe "the professionals will clean my clock." Nevertheless, none of these thoughts are accurate. This does not imply that options trading is elementary that anybody can do it. If you are a motivated student, trading options is not that difficult to learn. Though it is hard, practically anyone can learn how to trade options with a little effort. Let's illustrate this point by considering each of the other excuses separately.

If options trading has a bad rap, it got it as an outcome of the Crash of 1987. That single event has, to date, altered the way individuals price options. Throughout the crash, there were stories of some traders losing everything as a result of being brief "naked puts." Does that mean there is truth to the declaration that options are too dangerous?

Many people are comfortable owning stocks. Which trade brings higher risks?, owning 100 shares of XYZ stock or being short an XYZ put (which commands 100 shares of stock)? Would you be surprised to know that owning stock is, in fact, riskier? And would you be amazed to see that you have much better odds of earning money being short an out of the cash put than being long stock? The difference in the odds can be considerable and entirely unexpected to many people.

Perhaps you have taken time to do your homework and have discovered that option price models are typically based on either some form of the Black-Scholes model, which is a partial differential formula, or the binomial model, which is a decision tree-style design. As a retail options trader, you do not need to understand the calculus behind the designs. Your broker must supply you with all the calculus-induced models you require to trade effectively and successfully! And some do so at no charge to you!

For you to be effective at options trading, Instead of the calculus behind the price models, you need to understand the odds, or probability theory, behind options. You don't have to become a statistician. You simply need to understand a few fundamentals, which are dealt with in this book.

While it will require some time and effort to learn about trading options effectively, when you master the process, you can trade by committing about ten minutes each day to it.

I hope you will stick with me as we check out the world of options.

CHAPTER ONE

Why Trade Options?

Many people ask, "With lots of places to invest and with the complexity of the markets, would I not be better off, letting a professional manage my money rather than trying to trade options myself?" The reluctance to go into the world of self-directed investing is understandable. However, experiences in the world of investments have shown that no one takes care of your money like you do. Many money managers go through about three to six months training program, and they get off running and trading your hard-earned savings.

The next questions that come up are; "But options are so complex, am I not much better off just trading stocks?" and "How could I potentially contend with the options professionals?"

Being Strategic without Direction

If you put about three or more market experts or professionals in the room and ask, "Which of you can forecast market and specific stock direction the best?" you better be ready for the heated argument that will ensue. The economist will say she can because she understands the mechanisms that drive the market in the long term. The essential expert will tell you that everybody understands the market increases in the long run, but he can separate which stocks will go up one of the most. The technical expert will say, "Hey, people, the marketplace moves in two directions. And I can tell you when you will be near assistance or resistance levels, and when the Fibonaccis have retraced."

Often a hot topic of debate, research shows that market movement is mainly random in the long run. And this premise of random (Brownian) motion is, in fact, at the heart of every alternative pricing design.

If markets move arbitrarily, then how does anyone earn money in the markets? Well, markets move arbitrarily, but with a "favorable drift." This means that in the long run, nearly everyone who owns a diversified stock portfolio ought to generate income. Which quantity ought to be around what is understood as the "risk-free rate of return." Over the past 50 years, that has totaled up to a bit over 6.2 percent each year. Now, that's a fair little bit of modification so that you might do even worse with your cash. But you can likewise do better-- a lot better.

As the technical analyst said, the marketplace relocates two instructions. Over the past 50 years, the market (as represented by the S&P 500 index) has gone up on 52.89 percent of the days and down on 47.11 percent of the days. Why try to make money by guessing which stock will go up the most? Options permit you to benefit from movement in either direction or from no movement at all! To put it merely, options are strategic without being directional. You can earn money from virtually any situation if you craft your trade correctly.

A Word about Leverage

This is a concept that is often criticized. When leverage is used appropriately, it is one of the most effective methods of enhancing portfolio returns offered. Why are we talking about leverage, and how does it relate to options?

Leverage, simply put, is when you use borrowed money to enhance the return on your investment. It increases the risk of your portfolio. If you are to be effective at trading, you need to understand the fact that risk can be a definite idea. All monetary instruments are simply ways of moving risk. As long as you are "paid" more than you view your risk to be, risk-taking, therefore, becomes your means of making money. To put it simply, you need to stop thinking of risk as something to be avoided and start embracing risk as your process of generating income. It is half of the risk versus return trade-off that needs to play a part in every trade you make.

The types and amounts of risks you take on in your portfolio ought to depend on your specific circumstance. Inputs to this decision consist of how old you are, how capable you are at enduring drawdowns (and replacing those lost funds), how well you comprehend riskier trades, how many edges you view in the trade, and on and on. One compelling piece of information options gives you is how much risks the options market individuals as a whole perceive in a given trade. So, you have many investors' cumulative views at your disposal to help you.

Returning to leverage, you don't remember saying you wished to borrow any money, do you? Maybe your credit ranking is not up to snuff. Or possibly you simply do not want to make those monthly payments. No concerns! You have two means of accomplishing leverage with options without needing to submit yourself to a credit check each time you borrow and without receiving those big coupon books in the mail. When you open a margin portfolio margin account, you are, in reality, establishing a mechanism for borrowing money. You do not even need to ask to get from then on. Your broker will immediately provide you additional funds and charge your account only for interest on the quantity utilized if you go beyond the capital in the report.

More to the point is that options are levered instruments in and of themselves. If you wish to buy 100 shares of GOOGL (Google) stock ($ 590) in your IRA (no leverage), you would have to create around $59,000. However, for a mere $3,300, you could command the very same 100 shares for the next 189 days, by purchasing a Mar 15 600Call option. Sure, the option has a different risk profile as well as profit and loss profile, but above a specific cost ($ 633), you will fully take part in the stock's benefit. After 189 days, you will either require to cough up the rest of the money to hold the stock or sell out your options to secure your earnings without ever having to create the additional money. Now! Where else can you borrow that sort of money without a credit check?

Going a bit deeper into what options leverage implies to your returns, let's say GOOGL stock goes up to $650 at the expiration of the options. While it holds, you will make more cash with stock in this example, let's examine the ROC (return on capital) for each trade.

As you can see, the non-annualized ROCs for the two methods are10.17 percent for the stock purchase and 51.52 percent for the purchase of the call options. Rather a distinction! And one that may make a trade inGOOGL possible, thinking about not everyone has $59,000 to plunk down for 100 shares of stock! This is the power that options offer.

Multiply that power by the loan you automatically receive in your margin or portfolio margin account, and you have the structure for some returns!

Options Are a Decaying Asset.

You know the old saying that a new vehicle loses 30 percent of its value the second you drive it off the lot? That might be overemphasized a bit though, the principle is clear. Options are just like cars, though as an option's devaluation starts slow and speeds up, the more detailed it gets to completion of its "life." At least you can use vehicles while they diminish, but you can't drive your option to the shop with the aim of buying a gallon of milk or a cup of yogurt. So, what good are options? To the owner of an opportunity, its decay causes a little bit of impatience in the hope of seeing your option grow in price just before the collapse "gets you." To the seller of the option, who took on the risk of the brief option, decay is their friend. So why would you ever purchase an option if you know it will decay away in time and serve no practical purpose while doing so? Well, options are not quite that fundamental. There are two parts to the value of an option, and they are called intrinsic value and extrinsic value.

Another point needs to be made about the rotting nature of an option. When you acquire an option, you are paying more than the option is (inherently) worth at that time. To put it simply, you are spending some premium (typically called time premium or insurance premium) for the right such option offers. Let's take a look at an example. Let's say XYZ stock is trading for $ 48.50, and the $47 call is trading for $2.25. If you purchased the call, exercised it instantly, and sold the stock you received from the exercise, you would get $1.50 for your trouble, exclusive of fees. Let's walk through this. You get to buy the stock for $47 and offer it out at the market price of $48.50 when you exercise the $47 calls. That suggests you keep $1.50. This is your intrinsic value. However, you paid $2.25 for that call, so you are still out$0.75. This is the extrinsic value, or time premium, which you paid for. It is this quantity of $0.75 that will decay away unless the stock rallies. And if you purchase an out of the money option, it is all extrinsic value by meaning. This means that if you buy an option, your probability of making money from it is less than 50 percent. Why purchase it? A long option has limited loss (what you pay for it) and limitless revenue capacity.

CHAPTER TWO

Options Trading Strategy Tips to Earn Money

It's relatively simple for us to generate income by trading because 90%+ of our trades pay. It's crucial to restrict risks by trading a small number of contracts and liquidate your trades early. The trading option premium has a high statistical possibility of earnings. The following strategies will help you streamline your options trading career.

- **Limit Your Information Sources:** Do not check out a website like SeekingAlpha.com or see CNBC. Those are for home entertainment purposes and will not assist you in making money.

- **Create a Watch List**: Only trade a few stocks, and try to have positions on 4-5 underlying stocks at one time. Just keep things incredibly easy and neglect everything else. I hugely recommend that you narrow the number of stocks that you trade. If you have an account size of $20,000, you ought to just trade 1-2 stocks at one time.

- **Trade from Your Phone**: You can make all trades from your phone and not necessarily use any charting software application. Keep things easy because if you complicate matters, it'll negatively impact your returns.

- **Get Familiar with the Recent Trading Range**: Get comfortable with the new trading range on the stocks in your watch list. If the trades at the high end of the variety, sell a call. If it trades at the low end of the array, offer a put.

- **Trade Naked Options**: Contact your broker and demand the ability to trade naked options. It's a lot more secure and a lot easier to manage positions.
- **Sign up for Trade Alerts:** Receive real-time trade notifications so that you optimize your profits and lessen your mistakes.

Factors To Consider For Trading Options

1. High returns

With options, you can accomplish high returns. 100% to 400% is not unusual in a matter of weeks or perhaps days. With the higher rate of return, you likewise deal with higher risks.

2. You can earn money when the market is fluctuating up and down:
All you need is for the market to be moving. You pick either a Put or Call option based upon what you believe the marketplace is doing.

3. Options are inexpensive:

Options are indeed cheap. A couple of financial investments have this type of cost. You might restrict your losses by putting in a stop-loss order.

4. Leverage

When purchasing options, you make use of leverage. Generally, you acquire option contracts worth of 100. You are not the owner of the stock, and you own the right to buy or sell the stock at a given cost. You sell the option or purchase the option which serves as insurance coverage to the buyer or seller of stock. You use your 100 to 1.

If you wish to learn how to make money in options trading, the first step is to develop a strategy for options trading. Don't merely leap in blind, but take a while and think of your objectives and how you plan to attain them. Numerous portfolios don't consist of any options trading methods at all, but that's a mistake. There's a lot to get from this element of the market.

Limit your drawback and grow your potential for profit by approaching options without fear. Trading options does not need to be a complex process if you don't desire it to be. Buying options to keep up with the cost motions of future stocks enables you to reduce your threats while concurrently opening the door for endless revenues.

Options can likewise be used for hedging and giving your portfolio a little cushion. Think about it; you buy insurance when you buy new cars and truck or other essential items, why not consider protecting your portfolio with insurance? Hedging can function as the last hope if your portfolio gets to that point.

There are a couple of methods that financiers can approach options. Instead of just purchasing shares in stocks that you anticipate will rise in value, you can buy call options to increase your advantage.

CHAPTER THREE

What to Look for in a broker

Before you trade any financial instrument, you need to open a brokerage account. Indeed, that might require more paperwork! But for many, that is not the worst part. There are many terms and principles embedded in the documents that are foreign to a lot of new investors. And there are many warnings regarding the dangers of different types of investments. In reality, there are additional risk disclosures particular to options you need to check out and sign when you create an account that allows options trading. But what brokers do not alert you about are the risks that are inherent in selecting the right brokerage firm.

Banks Versus Brokerages

Many people are comfortable putting their money into banks. They ensure that when they drive to their local branch and ask for $300 to do some shopping, the bank will comply. They are also confident that when they decide to withdraw large portions of their accounts, the bank will not have an issue creating the funds. This is particularly true for bigger banks. In spite of some times of distress, such as the financial crisis of 2008-- 2009, the reality that the government-run FDIC (Federal Deposit Insurance Corporation) insures as much as an overall of

$250,000 for each deposit category in each insured bank provides additional security to the depositor. But what do banks do with your cash when you transfer it? If you are to be truly comfortable, shouldn't you understand what happens with it when you drop it off? Well, soon after you drop your money off, the bank is out loaning it to somebody else or some other business.

So, why am I telling you of the safety of your bank account when we are speaking about brokerages? Well, in my opinion, if you choose the proper brokerage, your cash is even more secure there. When you deposit funds in a brokerage account, your financial organization has a legal commitment to segregate your funds into a separate account for your advantage. In other words, your funds will not be at risk if Tom or Fred loses his task and can not repay his loans. Though the FDIC does not cover your account, it is, in fact, covered by SIPC (Securities Investor Protection Corporation). And it is covered for $500,000, $250,000 of which can be in cash. In total, it is included for twice that of your account. Of course, this security does not encompass trading losses or fraud. Instead, it covers you against your brokerage company going insolvent due to less dubious reasons. SIPC is not a government-run corporation. It is funded by the member companies that are covered by SIPC. So, though SIPC exists to secure you, just as when you pick a bank, there is no reason to lure fate. You do not want to depend on the "safeguard" under your account. Let's look at more steps you should consider to secure your money.

Depth of a Broker's Pockets

Just as the small, local bank down the street is luring but fails to have as much "room for mistake" as the big bank in town, a big brokerage firm is usually a safer bet with less threat of losing your funds. Initially, large brokerages, by meaning, have deeper pockets. Hence, just as JP Morgan Chase was able to quickly hold up against losses from the "London Whale's" trading as a result of its deep pockets, a large brokerage can also stand up to damages triggered by errors. Even big brokerages do not start as large institutions. They have paid their dues and are usually run by experienced industry experts with knowledge far beyond those of most small firms. They have also "vetted" their policies to be sure they are safe and correct and operate in all (or virtually all) market conditions. More prominent companies also generally have instituted what we call "business risk management policies and procedures." These are created to add security against all recognized threats to the company.

Trading Risk Management

If you have been around floor traders for any length of time, one remark you may have heard is, "My cleaning company's risk managers are a pain in my ass!". This is one point in which it appears professional traders are misguided. A market breakdown could then put the firm at risk of losses beyond their ability to cover, thereby putting everyone's money at risk.

Account Types

There are numerous ways to categorize account types. This section of the book will focus on the three models that apply to options trading. For our purposes, we will categorize accounts as the following:

1. Cash

2. Reg-T Margin

3. Portfolio Margin

Cash Accounts

Perhaps the most common type of cash account is an IRA. You can get permission from your broker to trade options with the following restrictions:

- All option purchases must be paid completely.
- You can never be short stock or short naked calls.
- When you trade a covered call, your stock is restricted.
- All option sales must be backed in cash up to the maximum loss possible.

Since options are levered instruments in and of themselves, the ability to trade options in a cash account vaults your account type into the category of a "partial margin account." This is just semantics, so do not get puzzled. Your IRA is still tax-deferred

Reg-T Margin Accounts

Unlike a cash account, where all securities must be paid for, ultimately, a margin account enables an investor to borrow money from his broker to cover the expense of the security (for long options) or to cover the threat of the security (for short options). Regulation T limits the amount obtained toward the trade to no higher than 50 percent.

Some people would ask: "Doesn't that increase your risk?" Margin can increase your risk by allowing you to put on more trades than you would otherwise have the ability to make without a loan. If you diversify your portfolio correctly, it does not always have to increase your risk. The act of levering will increase your return on capital, as long as you pay.

Portfolio Margin Accounts

In April 2007, the SEC started permitting portfolio margining in retail accounts. For portfolio margin accounts, the margin is calculated based upon the total risk in the portfolio. This indicates if trades have offsetting risk, margin can really drop as you include trades. The margin is determined each night by the OCC (Options Clearing Corp.), using a system known as the "TheoreticalIntermarket Margining System" (TIMS). This system calculates the most significant potential loss for all positions (in aggregate) in an item class across a variety of underlying volatilities and rates. That margin amount usually is less than that calculated by the Reg-T margin system. And once again, position margin is not additive but rather determined as a total portfolio, thus offering the account type its name.

One point about portfolio margin accounts you must know. Many portfolio margin accounts have much higher minimum capital requirements than do margin accounts. At my broker, you can open a Reg-T margin account with as little as $2,000, while a portfolio margin account needs a minimum of $125,000. Some brokers will require you to pass an examination displaying your understanding of margining and trading before allowing you access to a portfolio margin account. Though there are advantages to a portfolio margin account, they are not for everyone and are controlled for the higher good of the broker's customers.

Overall, more recent options traders ought to be looking to open a margin account, while knowledgeable traders that qualify need to want to open a portfolio margin account. You do not always need to use the increased leverage offered, but it is good to have access to it when a situation for which it is helpful develops.

Commissions

Commissions of all kinds are the expense of working. Lots of traders will go shopping brokerages based upon fees alone. This is a bit short-sighted for some reason. Initially, we will go over the kinds of commissions that brokerages charge, and after that, we will discuss their ramifications for our trading and our choice of brokers.

Commissions are typically charged in three ways:

1. A per deal charge up to a certain number of agreements.

2. A ticket charge plus a per agreement charge.

3. Per agreement charge alone.

The very first type, a fixed price, per transaction charge, is uncommon in the options world. It is a lot more familiar with stocks where you may be able to trade approximately 1,000 shares of stock for a set charge, and even limitless shares per deal for a set fee. These kinds of setups may be excellent for someone who trades stock in big chunks. But for a more recent trader who is trading ina little account, I would highly recommend staying away from this kind of structure. Let's look at an example where you are charged $7 per deal, and you generally trade 100 shares of stock per trade. That would exercise to $.07 per share in and $.07 out, which means you need to make $.14 per trade just to break even.

Moving back to the options world, the equivalent of this type of structure is the "ticket charge plus deal cost" setup. Using an example, you may be provided a $7.95 ticket charge plus $0.75 per agreement cost. This indicates that for each option deal you make, you will be charged $7.95, plus $0.75 times the variety of contracts carried out in your order. If you trade one contract, your fee is $8.70 (($ 7.95 + (1 $0.75)). For 10 contracts, your commission would be $15.45 (($ 7.95 + (10 $0.75)), or $1.545 per agreement. If you trade 50 agreements in your order, your charge would be $45.45 (($ 7.95 + (50 0.75)), or $0.909 per agreement.

An alternative may be to sustain a per contract cost only. That fee, for new accounts, might be $1.50 per contract. As you can see, if you are trading one agreement per trade, you would be far better off with this structure as you will be paying $1.50 per trade instead of $8.70 per trade. As a 50-contract trader, you may be better off with the mixed structure, but my guess is that if your typical contract size is 50 contracts, you might get your per deal charge down low enough to wish still to avoid ticket charges.

Among the fascinating things to note is that brokerages will often attempt to force new traders to have a ticket charge. This ensures the brokerage will make cash on each deal, even if you do not! This is backward, as a new trader will cease to be an options trader at all with those types of fees. After all, if you are starting to trade and are selling a $1 enormous credit spread for $0.35, and your commissions are $8.70 to put it on and $8.70 to close the trade, your optimum revenue is now ($ 0.35-- (2 $8.70)) or$ 0.176, while your prospective loss is ($ 0.65 + (2 * $8.70)) or $0.824.

With your likelihood of profiting at around 65 percent, these trades are practically assurances; you will lose cash over time. I suggest not opening an account at a brokerage that insists on a ticket charge. The majority of brokerages, but not all, will negotiate this. If the one you are taking a look at will not, it is time to take a look at another company.

Presuming you have opened an account and picked a fixed commission schedule, I just want to put commissions in perspective. They are variable costs (i.e., expenses you sustain only when you make a trade) that can positively affect your success, there are other considerations that offset and, in my view, far surpass the commission schedule's value.

We will deal with a lot of them in more detail later in the book, however, for your factor to consider:

- Trading liquid options with tight bid/ask spreads have a much higher result on your profitability than commissions. Here is an example. Let's state you are trading a relatively illiquid stock called XYZ. The option you want to offer is priced estimate

$3.40 bid at $3.70 deal. If you need to quit $0.30 getting in and out because of the bid/ask spread, you are genuinely getting $30 per contract, due to the options "100 share" multiplier. Contrast this with the distinction between a $1.50 and a $1.00 commission structure per share, and you will rapidly see the bid/ask spread in this example is 60 times larger.

- Of course, your option of which options you choose to trade, and therefore the width of the bid/ask spread, is relatively untouched by your option of brokers. However, your broker's ability to get your orders filled somewhere in the middle of the spread is of substantial importance.

- Back to that robust front-end system: Having a trading system that assists in finding and handling your trades is also of substantial importance. What good are cheap commissions if you can not discover a way to make money trading?

- Data feeds can be expensive. Brokers charge a monthly cost to their customers as a means of recovering their costs of information acquisition. Others will take in those costs as a cost of doing organization. Depending on how frequently you trade, this might be a significant consideration for you. If you get lower commissions, however, have to pay data-feed fees, you may be paying more in the long run. You are exchanging variable costs for fixed expenses.

- There is nothing more frustrating than trading in a slow market for several years, and then, when you eventually have an active market, your broker's systems can not maintain, and you fail to make the most of a golden opportunity. This reliability, when again, can be much more crucial than a 25 or 50-cent reduction in commissions.

CHAPTER FOUR

Phases of the Market

This chapter will check out the cost patterns that continuously come back in the market and talk about the participants that produce the models. It handles not only the designs themselves but the psychology of the marketplace participants and why the action of the traders exposes itself in the continuously duplicating patterns.

We understand mathematically that when a trade occurs, the marketplace needs to be in balance. When the trade occurs, the rate can go anywhere. This chapter is written to help explain the market in different phases. The terms used are not universal in any way but are vital to this study. Some people have different names used for them, but for this book, we will use the definitions as stated below;

■Congestion

I believe that all liquid markets have the same cycle. It does not matter what the hidden asset that is going to be traded; it will go through a period. I think that the preliminary phase of any market is congestion.

When the participants are confused by congestion is the section of the cycle, the current price action. The long and the brief traders will exchange positions as the steady hands continuously change. If you are a short-term trader, this can happen as numerous as five or six times throughout a session. Unless you are a countertrend trader (selling as rate advances and buying when it decreases, likewise called the weak hands), trading in this kind of market can be aggravating. You might purchase a number of tops and offer a variety of bottoms. This is known as getting whipsawed, and it is one of the problems of being a reactive trader. Another name for reactive traders is trend following. They search for the direction that cost is moving and then use technical analysis to" follow the pattern." I am not a stringent pattern trader; however, instead, react to the current market stage.

When the market starts to whipsaw, I continuously lose cash on the first set of trades. The congestion stage is marked initially by fictional limits called support and resistance. It might assist in believing in relief as the floor of the market, and that resistance is the ceiling.

Support is where the weak hands will balance down and buy additional shares of stock or agreements to reduce their average cost. It is also the position where traders who have been observing the existing market will make a buy. If the support holds, the long traders will become the steady hands, and the shorts (weak hands) will be required to either take profit or begin to cover their loss and look for a new area to get in. They will press the market to the other side, and it will start to find some resistance if the new purchasers are strong enough.

Resistance will bring sellers back to the market, countertrend traders will" average up," and the shorts offer additional shares or contracts to raise their typical sale. The resistance will also restore traders who have been observing, and they will start to provide. If the strongholds, the short traders will become the steady hands, and the marketplace will force the long traders (now the weak hands) either to take profit or lock in their loss. They will push the market back to test the support a 2nd time if the sellers are strong enough.

This test is understood as a double bottom. It is significant, as it will be among the most profitable trades that you make in weekly options. If the double bottom holds, it will bring more buyers into the market, and the sellers will begin to take profit or lock-in loss. The strong hands will now be the buyers, and they will take the cost back to the previous resistance. If that point holds, it will become a double top, and it is hugely significant as the blockage area will now be defined.

As long as the market remains in the congestion pattern, it will be traded the same way of buying the double bottoms and selling the double tops. Congestion can last for a very long time. If you purchase every day, it might last for months, even longer.

It might continue some days or weeks if you are a day trader or a swing trader. Many specialists believe that market is in congestion more than 60 percent of the time. They hit on the exact top and bottom. Fundamentalists state that this pattern is a self-fulfilling prophecy; professionals say that traders recognize this pattern and adapt their trading style to take advantage of it. Undoubtedly, I agree with the professionals. The breakout took place when the long traders from the 3rd double bottom (triple quadruple; I always use double) in a row held, and they forced the sellers out at the next double top.

■ Breakout to the Trend

When the previous support and resistance levels fail to hold, the breakout to the trend will start. The double top and double bottom sellers will begin to feel pressure when their standards are violated; they know that breakout and pattern traders will be entering into the market as new cash. This imbalance will begin to generate more buyers or sellers, forcing the countertrend traders to abandon positions. When the market makes its first more significant high or lower low, the culmination of the purchasing or swelling will occur. Profit takers will enter the market, and they might be signed up with a wave of countertrend traders that might force the cost below/above the old support or resistance levels. If that happens, it would be entitled to a false breakout. After the low is made, the marketplace made a series and reversed lower highs and higher lows. When the double leading failed to hold, the rate ultimately rallied back into the congestion phase and broke out to the pattern on the benefit.

When the profit taking subsides, if a more significant low or a lower high holds, the trend is confirmed. The market never goes in one direction permanently; even in a pattern, there will be some price motion to the opposite of the trending market as profit taking and countertrend traders will continue to try and move price in their favor—the upward or down angle at which the trend.

Most of trending markets can not sustain a price rise/fall on an angle of over 45 degrees. As you can observe, the price meanders around the mean as profit taking and countertrend traders take their piece out of the pie.

Eventually, the marketplace will make a high/low that has a lower high or more significant low follow it on the next cost swing. This is the first indication that the trend may be reversing. A market is pausing before it resumes its pattern, or the present trend may be ending. The strong hands that had been managing the market will become the weak hands, and when this occurs, it will reenter the congestion stage. The brand-new congestion might be a breather, and the fight between the steady hands and the weak hands may solve itself in a breakout back to the previous significant trend. If the market is making a rounding top or bottom, the new congestion stage will cause a breakout to the opposite side of the existing pattern, and a brand-new trending phase will begin to the reverse side of the current market.

■ Blowoff

If the current trend doesn't resolve itself in a rounding top/bottom and costs begin to accelerate at a much steeper angle than the sustainable 45-degree rate, the market will more than likely end in a blowoff. The blowoff phase of the marketplace is always the least quantity of time in any of the three steps; however, it might lead to the absolute rate movement. When the weak hands get squeezed to the limitation, the blowoff takes place. They can no longer fight the trend, and they are forced to cover, probably through the absence of capital or margin calls that should be satisfied. During the blowoff rate, phase and time may become infinite; meaning rate reaches a vertical relocation of 90 degrees. Every tick is either higher or lower, the weak hands end up being price-insensitive, and the only thing they show exciting is getting enough amount to end the discomfort. The degree of the blowoff draws in new cash to the old, weak hands' now-vacated position. The strong hands begin to take profit. They might also join the brand-new money in altering instructions. When this happens, the classic V pattern is formed in the market. Ultimately, the marketplace goes back to stability, and a new market pattern starts.

The vital principle provided is that in a liquid market, the significant rate patterns offered in this area can be depended on to repeat with regular frequency. They might have elements linked, as in the examples of a blowoff resulting in another blowoff, however, the one thing they share is that they are mathematically ensured to repeat.

CHAPTER FIVE

Call Options Versus Put Options

Put options

It's essential to understand the various kinds of options when trying to make money trading options. There are two primary kinds of options, call options and put options. Both are a kind of contract. These option contracts include two parties, the option holder and the option issuer. The option holder is conferred with the right to perform a specific transaction with the issuer, but the holder isn't required to carry out that deal.

Call options manage the right to buy and put options to afford the right to sell. The strike cost is the agreed-upon rate for the property under contract. In stock trading, the property is the share. A call option offers the option holder the right to buy a share or shares at a strike rate for an identified period. When the time is up, the contract hits its expiration date and becomes worthless. A put option offers the option holder the right to sell shares at a strike cost for a set amount of time.

If an investor believes the worth of shares will rise, they purchase call options. If they understand the value will fall, they buy put options. The ability to properly check out an options chain is essential to succeed in buying and selling options at earnings.

Benefits of Trading Call Options

In addition to making more money with options trading, you can also take advantage of the way they function when it comes to risks.

The majority of equity options and index option contracts in the United States benefit one month and end on the third Friday of that month. As the stock exchange continues to adjust to changes, more transactions are altering this rule and providing option contracts with weekly expiration dates for a quicker turn-around on more significant stocks and indices.

American call options offer a fair bit of versatility compared to European options. A trader can implement their call option agreements at any time before the deal expires with American style options. Still, European style options need the trader to wait until the expiration date to enforce the agreement.

Call options likewise offer limitless earning possible with minimal risk for loss.

If you acquire a call option contract for $1 per show, a strike cost of $10 per share, and the price rises to $1000; your call options would have an intrinsic worth of $900 per share, leaving you with huge earnings.

If they drop to $0 per share, you'll just lose what you spent on the contract. Say you buy an agreement for 100 shares. That's a loss capacity of $100 with a revenue potential of more than $90,000.

Five Reasons Why Options Trading Is Better Than Stock Trading

Options trading has been the center of much debate of current years. Is it dangerous? Can we declare bankruptcy? Indeed, options being a form of the derivative instrument are even more complex than the stocks that they are composed based upon and, like a wild stallion, can harm you if you do not know how it works and how to use it properly.

I will provide five reasons options trading is much better than stock trading to resolve the age-old misconceptions of how unsafe options trading is. Let's remember this: Options trading threatens just when you do not comprehend it.

1) Variable Leverage

The take advantage those options give you is possibly the primary reason that people gravitate to options trading in the first place. Trading options enables you to make a lot more earnings on the same carry on the underlying stock. You are merely making 1% revenue on a 1% relocation in your favor when you purchase the stock itself without margin.

Nevertheless, in options trading, you could be making 10% revenue on that same 1% relocation the stock made or even as much as 100% on that same 1% relocation!

Yes, the charm of leverage in options, unlike in futures trading, is that it is FLEXIBLE!

You could handle more leverage for more danger or lower take advantage for lower-danger by picking options of different strike costs and expiration month.

This explains why the beauty of leverage in options trading is that it permits you to make the same trades with much lesser cash; as such, you could simply use only cash you can pay for to and mean to lose in any unsuccessful business for each options trade. Hence, leverage helps you manage your losses significantly!

2) Low Capital Required

Apple Inc., AAPL, is trading at over $295.36 today, which implies it takes $29,536 to purchase 100 shares today. However, AAPL's at the cash call options cost something like $715 to control the earnings on that same 100 shares of Apple!

3) Bet Downwards Without Margin

You might only short the stock, which sustains margin. However, in trading options, all you need to do to bank on a stock moving downwards is to BUY its put options with no margin required at all. That's right; purchasing put options for earnings to drawback works the purchasing call options for revenue to upside precisely. There is no significant need to own the stock ahead of time, and there is no requirement for margin!

4) Multi-Directional Profits

In stock trading, you only make money when the stock goes in the directions you desire it to. There is no other way to benefit in both circumstances simultaneously, and there is no chance to make a profit if the price of the stock does not move. However, in options trading, such multi-directional earnings are possible! There are options methods that allow you to benefit no matter if the stock goes upwards or downwards quickly, and there are options strategies that profit even if the cost of the capital stays unchanged! Such is the real magic of options methods, which significantly increases your opportunities of winning in options trading versus stock trading!

5) Play Banker

Tired and ill of always being at the player's side of the table? In options trading, you could switch instead to the banker's side of the table and do what market makers do by offering options to individuals who are desires to take the bottom of the player! When the players lose, as they typically do, you get to keep the bet as earnings much like a real banker! Just options trading has the "bet," which you get to follow and it is known as "extrinsic worth."

CHAPTER SIX

Trade Probabilities: What to Look For

•Interest Rates

We spoke earlier about margin accounts. With those accounts, your broker will instantly loan you cash when you have surpassed the quantity of money available in your account. That advantage does not come free of charge. Your broker will have to charge you interest on the funds you borrow. Not all brokers reveal this to you; it appears to surprise many newer traders when they suddenly have an interest charge hit their accounts at the end of a month. And comparable to our conversation on commissions, the rates charged usually are less considerable than other issues.

Stock Borrow and Loan

Stock obtain and loan might not be a very crucial topic for you most of the time if you are continually trading extremely liquid stocks and options. Sometimes (like after specific corporate actions), a share in which you have a position might end up being hard, or impossible, to borrow. Let's talk about a couple of terms, and after that, examine how picking a great broker might make your life much more comfortable.

Shorting Stock

Individuals new to trading are typically confused and shocked by the principle of "shorting a stock." Shorting a stock is when you offer stock you do not presently own. How can you offer something you do not own? By obtaining it from someone else, naturally. It is not like you are borrowing your next-door neighbor's lawnmower and delivering it to a person across town. That may make your neighbor a bit upset. Stocks are more generic. That is, one share of XYZ stock is the same as any other share of XYZ stock (offered we are mentioning the very same class of stock). Your broker discovers someone to borrow the stock from on your behalf and permits you to provide it with. Why would you do that? You will do that if you think the price of the stock is too high and wish to benefit from its going back to a more "reasonable" cost. You "sell" it now, and you must repurchase it later in the day and time to "return" it to the lending institution of the stock. Once again, the borrowing and returning are all done by your broker and are transparent to you. What could go incorrect if this is all done behind the scenes? Why speak about it at all, aside from to say it is a normal part of stock trading? We are getting to that!

Easy to Borrow

In normal circumstances, everything goes efficiently with the stock obtain and loan activity. Every trading day, your broker finds every stock that you receive in anticipation, or another customer, may have the desire to do so. When the stock is readily available, that is easy to obtain. That indicates you can short the stock without any issues. Usually, this is reflected via your broker's trading software by a lack of any tagging. Some brokers might tell you it is easy to borrow (ETB), but typically it is an absence of notice that tells you all is well.

Hard to Borrow

There are times when lots of people, all viewing the very same image, come to the same conclusion. Individuals who are going long might offer their stock (and might even go short the stock) if that conclusion is that the stock is overpriced. By providing their stock, they no longer have stock to offer. Individuals who have no position might select to brief also. The schedule of stock to borrow begins to diminish, and the stock ends up being "hard to obtain." When a stock is tough to acquire, it will be assessed your trading software, and if you wish to short the stock, you will most likely require to have direct communication with your broker. The broker will search further for you to find the stock. At times, they might offer to lock up stock for you for a fee. This charge is reflected by an interest rate you should pay to hold the stock aside for you to obtain versus. Your trade now handles a new risk/return ratio for you to consider before moving forward.

- Impossible to Borrow

When there is no stock available to borrow at (virtually) any rate, we call this stock "impossible to obtain." You can not short this stock. Your trading software application will stop you. Your broker, somewhere on their website, releases a list of impossible-to-borrow stocks for your perusal every day.

- Buy-Ins

What happens if you short a stock when it is easy to obtain but later becomes impossible to achieve? By law, your broker can not allow you to remain brief the stock if the stock that your broker borrowed in your place gets pulled away (either offered or the owner simply refuses to lend any more). Your broker looks around for brand-new sources of stock to obtain and shows up empty. You are now based on what we call a "buy-in." This suggests that later in the trading day, the broker will buy some or all of your stock back on your behalf and location it in your account. Your short position will be decreased or end at the price your broker chooses to pay.

- Short Interest

One method to anticipate the problem you may have in borrowing stock is to track a stock's short interest. "Short interest" is specified as the difference of shares sold briefly and not yet repurchased. If you sell shares you own, this does not impact the short interest. If you sell shares you do not own (short the stock), this sale gets shown in the brief interest number. How can you interpret the short interest number? There are two methods, either of which can be utilized to raise a warning.

Let's say XXX stock has a short interest of 6 million shares, and ZZZ stock has a short interest of 24 million. Does this mean shorting ZZZ stock has more threat than shorting XXX stock? Not necessarily. There are two different aspects in which we can compare the short interest number to evaluate our risk.

Initially, we can compare this number to the stock's float. A stock's float describes the number of shares that are offered to be purchased and provided by the general investing public. By dividing the short interest into the raft, we get a reading as to the portion of offered shares that are presently provided short. We can get a stock's float from a variety of commercial sites (such as yahoo. finance.com), as it is an extensively recognized and distributed number.

Returning to our example, if XXX stock has a float of 24 million shares, its short interest is 25 percent. If ZZZ has a raft of 480 million shares, its short interest is 5 percent. So, XXX would have a more significant buy-in threat, all other things being equal.

We can also look up the stock's "days to cover" number. Days to cover describes the stock's short interest divided by the daily volume of the capital. This offers you an idea of how hard it might be for brief sellers to purchase back their stock. When the days to cover begins to approach near double digits, one gets worried and will frequently aim to start paring back the short position.

Where Your Broker Matters

Why go over all this in a section called "Stock Borrow and Loan"? As soon as you have gone through a buy-in, you will most likely say you would rather have a root canal. You will do everything you can to avoid another. A large, trusted broker will have a large stock, and many relationships forged that will give it much better access to stock availability for loaning. Size isn't the only factor to consider; size and credibility frequently play critical roles in your broker's capacity to borrow stock on your behalf.

Trading Platforms

Some brokers have numerous platforms, one for frequent traders (and experts) and another for the typical retail trader. If you do not fall into the first classification, I would be wary of accepting the "dumbed down" platform. Unless the broker can encourage you that they are streamlining your life by protecting you from unwanted information, it appears they are telling you you're a second-class resident who might not use and discover the tools other "smarter" traders use. An excellent front-end trading system should do this few things at a minimum:

1. Must be easy to use and provide excellent methods to learn the platform

2. Enable you to see historical options and stock data

3. Have a mobile platform offered

When shopping for a broker, you need to think about a lot more than merely commissions. Consider your broker as your partner in the organization. When searching for a partner, do you look for the cheapest option, or do you find the one who adds one of the most value? Defend the very best commission structure you can get, however, only after thinking about all the other worth propositions offered by each broker. In my opinion, 25 or 50 cents per agreement differential in commissions. As a number of the traders, state, "You do not understand what you don't know." Until you have dealt with many platforms, had to handle different firms on buy-ins, or had your trading platform shut down during busy market conditions, you have a little conceptual basis for these decisions. I hope you at least now have a better concept of the concerns you ought to ask and what value you need to get from your broker.

CHAPTER SEVEN

Making Profit From Trading Options

Different elements can affect an option's cost, so traders can't anticipate to start purchasing call options and making revenues simply. Only particular trades will end in a receipt for the buyer; others will cause a loss. A trader will just successfully benefit from trading call options when they buy options for a stock that is anticipated to increase at a decent rate over the following week or month.

Consider how much you anticipate the stock to rise. This is where excellent research enters play. Understanding a specific option's history and prepare for their future is vital to earning a profit.

Buying out-of-the-money call options for a $50 strike price isn't a great move if the cost is just most likely to increase 5 cents per day. However, if the stock is most likely to move as much as 50 cents per day, it has the potential to be a terrific play. The volatility also plays a significant role in whether it's an excellent concept to purchase its options. Some people take pleasure in the thrill, but a lucrative trader represents the market thoroughly and does not take numerous substantial threats.

Although lots of traders only purchase out-of-the-money options, like we said in the past, this isn't, in fact, a powerful technique. OTM options do use low costs, so they have the capacity for some severe turn-around. However, they're risky. Some traders much like the concept of owning several options, so they 'd instead buy a lot of more affordable OTM options than a couple of strong ones.

Think about whether you play the lottery. Possibly trading in OTM options is something you 'd delight in if you do. The options exchange shouldn't be performed like the lotto. The odds don't have to be wrong. Play it smart and offer yourself excellent odds.

Ways to Improve Your Options Trading

Here are actionable steps you can begin today to improve your options trading:

1. Find Out and Master Options Trading Fundamentals

You must understand the basics of options before you venture out option trades. It must be followed by orderly. It's the reason that we discover how to do basic math and subtraction before we go into the department and multiplication.

You require to know whatever about "puts" and "calls"-- from how they work and when it's finest to use them. This likewise consists of understanding everything related to them like expiration dates to where they are found on the first option tables. Skimming the essentials to enter into more innovative trading is just betting.

2. Read Books on Options Trading

Technically, they don't need to be everything about options trading, given that there is overlap in every investment book. The objective is to discover various methods of trading the market. You'll find out about things you have not understood about before, and you'll even be able to improve your initial trading method.

One excellent benefit derived from reading books is that you can also find out more about the covert trading elements you do not see daily like investor psychology or market psychology. Did you understand that these psychologies are the reason that technical analysis exist?

3. Streamline Your Technical Analysis

You're most likely doing yourself a disservice if you are looking at 6+ more technical indications and use multiple technical analyses concepts versus other technical analyses concepts.

Just learn and use the fundamentals like MACD, support/resistance, trending channels, divergence/convergence, and moving averages.

4. Continue to Paper Trade

Because you are trading genuine money, it doesn't suggest you require to stop learning and attempting out different techniques, just. You have to keep on playing the market from all angles. You can try a contrarian method if you are a market conformist (you tend to go with the trend) If you usually close out credit spreads, try keeping one open while legging in an OTM put option.

Experiment and continue to fine-tune out your strategy.

One excellent suggestion is to develop two similar trades—one in your routine account and the other in your paper trading account at the very same time. You can make experimental changes to your paper account over time and see how it fairs against the live account. This is a cool way you can test different techniques while having a baseline.

5. Select an Option Trade That You Love and Master It

A fantastic way to enhance your options trading is by mastering a support trade. Learn all the ins and outs of your practice by back-testing historical data, checking present conditions using paper trades, and checking out your favorite sell books.

When you understand the intricacies of your go-to trade, then you'll be able to better acknowledge scenarios and markets that your trade will thrive in. In turn, you'll receive a higher probability of success and earnings.

The secret is to stay with the first trade like an iron condor or credit spread—no innovative layered trades.

6. Adhere to Your Trading Plan

All successful traders have a trading plan. This suggests, they have a strategy to enter a trade, make changes, and exit positions based upon SPECIFIC occasions. Successful traders DO NOT make arbitrary decisions. Everything they do is determined, measured, and examined.

You can make an easy-to-follow trading formula based on technical analysis if you wish to as well.

7. Await Opportunities

This is a massive issue for newbie traders. It was even an issue for me when I started trading. I would have a couple of stocks on my watchlist that I wished to get into. However, I knew it wasn't the correct time. When I'm not looking, the stock takes off, and then. On a few celebrations, I have chased after stocks that ultimately turned against me.

These kinds of situations hurt in 2 methods: 1) damages your ego, and 2) dents your portfolio balance.

If you have the very same problems, don't worry. Luckily, it's been well recorded that reliable yearly portfolio efficiency is typically brought on by having a strong exit strategy.

8. File and Learn From Your Previous Trades

Every trade is a finding out experience. Do not focus solely on losing trades; however, also look at your winners. There is always something you can discover.

For losing trades, look into why the trade lost or possible ways you could have avoided it from happening. Examine your entry, the adjustments you made, the exit, and the total market behavior.

For winning trades, look into why the trade won, and possible methods you might have even benefited more. Evaluate your entry, the changes you made, the exit, and the total market habits.

It's the same analysis for both types of trades if you see. After a couple of trades, you'll begin to acknowledge crucial attributes to why some trades win and why some trades lose. From there, you can recognize what adjustments need to be made to mitigate a loss or increase revenue gain.

9. Continue to Learn From Successful Traders that STILL Trade

They will frequently look over your shoulder and guarantee that you are setting yourself up for the best trade possible for the existing market when you have a mentor. You'll understand that their guidance is sound when you see them trading their suggestions.

I find that it's entirely wrong to receive trading guidance from someone that doesn't trade themselves. If you don't think you need on-going options trading education and assistance, ask yourself these questions:

- Why do expert athletes have coaches?

- Why do Fortune 500 companies employ consultants?

- Why does the President have advisers?

The answer to all of these concerns is basic:

Coaches hold you accountable, assist you to specify & reach objectives, are on the outside looking in, and they can provide a wealth of understanding when dealing with the subject at hand. Basically, coaches assist you progress traders.

Profit By Keeping to Your Plan

Leaving money in options is a waste of your properties if the waiting isn't going to make you an earnings. The safest technique is to make your trade as quickly as revenue is available. Plenty fall into the temptation of greed by earning much, but waiting too long might soon result in you kicking yourself since you lost an opportunity.

Before purchasing an option, make a strategy. You must choose on a target earnings with your plan. As quickly as your option hits that target, make the trade. Stick to your guns. Even if the goal is struck early on in the contract period, make the trade

Earnings By Knowing the Factors

One of the key elements to profiting from options trading is having a mutual understanding of the stock market and its current trends. Individual stocks do not move entirely out of touch with the market.

Understanding every aspect that impacts a stock before you purchase its options is the very best way to manage your threat. Don't delve into any decisions blindly or ill-informed. Normally, more expensive options are less most likely to make you a profit, so beware when accepting your option contracts.

We desire you to succeed. A lot of new-to-the-scene traders jump into the game without cautioning or much understanding. The more you understand, the more active you are likely to be. Find out more about trading by joining our Free Bootcamp now! The specialists at RagingBull are here to inform and assist you in reaching your full trading potential

CHAPTER EIGHT

Choosing Your Trades

Now that we have considered the probability formulas and theoretical background, you may be questioning, "What good is all the details, and how can it help me to generate income?" I'm thankful you asked, as it's time to put this theoretical background to use. There is no guarantee that a provided trade will pay. If we can develop a methodology that takes advantage of what we know about an options trade, we can make money in the long run. Taking benefit of the probabilities is crucial to our success.

Selecting Your Underlying

Before you can search for trades, it is essential that you produce a list of underlying that you like to trade. This list needs to consist of liquid items that have adequate volume and open interest to make sure of an efficient market. If the quote/ ask spread is too broad, you might be quitting any edge you battled so tricky to accomplish. The list needs to be long enough to provide you sufficient underlying to trade, yet brief adequate to filter out any "sound" and provide you with only viable trading prospects. Additionally, I like to be familiar with every one of the underlying I trade. I advise you to begin with a much shorter list of core trading prospects and include new underlying as you are able.

The very first action in lining up a trade is to choose an underlying that you feel will provide you a probability edge. We now take a look at a variety of processes that will help us in this mission.

From a simplified viewpoint, if our objective is to buy low and offer high, or to provide high and then buy low, we need to determine which inputs of options rates have the most significant effect and are of the most considerable importance. Recalling at the data into the Black-Scholes design, we can rapidly dismiss rates of interest and dividend (both foundation of our standard calculation), as they are relatively static in nature days to expiration, but essential when we pick a technique, have little effect on our choice of underlying, as time passes equally for all. The same can be stated for strike cost, as that is also part of the strategy we choose and not part of our option of underlying. That leaves us with two inputs that will mainly drive the success or failure of any offered trade. These two inputs are stock rate and implied volatility.

Let's first take a look at the stock rate and its effect on our choice of underlying. If you have an understanding of the option Greeks that are originated from the option rates model, you will understand that the option's delta forecasts the change in an alternative price for each \$1 move in its underlying. Eventually, it is, in fact, the motion of the underlying that has the best influence on whether a trade is successful. Why do we invest so much energy and time talking about an option's implied volatility? To answer this, let's spend a few minutes to think of the ramifications of making trades entirely around our forecasts for the underlying's future movement.

The concern that must be responded to is whether you can regularly predict the instructions and magnitude of a stock's motion within a particular timespan. An option has a restricted life expectancy. We will discuss this in more information; later on, we must consider this reality now. If you think XYZ stock will rise in the future, that belief alone is not adequate to require purchasing a call choice with 30 days left till expiration. You need to, in truth, think XYZ will increase higher than a certain amount within the next 30 days for that details to be beneficial in your options trading. Does that mean we should disregard our beliefs about what a stock will perform in the future? It is tough to consistently predict a stock's instructions and magnitude of move within a given amount of time.

There is a term you might often hear used in financing, which name is "mean reversion." Some analysts will state a stock's price is mean going back. Simply put, what goes up need to boil down. When we speak of a stock's rate, there is little evidence to support this claim. For instance, even if we talk about a stock's rate movement being random, we quickly also to assert the stock's cost distribution has a favorable drift. That means that a reasonable stock price will drift up with time. In truth, if we think about stocks like Lucent or WorldCom, we acknowledge that some stocks may not just fail to drift upward but also, in truth, go to zero. That is, these businesses may declare bankruptcy, clearly breaking our upward drift theory. The point I am making is that stock prices usually are not as mean going back as many individuals believe. I find that thinking about stock prices as being mean reverting in the short term often gets in the way of developing a regularly rewarding options trading approach.

Why speak about mean reversion at all if I do not believe stock rates are mean-reverting? Well, in truth, I believe implied volatility is among the most mean reverse functions we see in finance. Let's take a better take a look at this statement.

Bring up a stock chart that spans one, two, three, or five years, for any ten underlying that pop into your head. As you move from one chart to the other, you will probably discover numerous charts that do not have a specified top end and bottom end within which the stock's price oscillates. On the other hand, if you bring up a suggested volatility chart for the same underlying with the same amount of time, you will most likely see that the implied volatility tends to oscillate within a variety. Looking more closely at these charts, you should be able to recognize a much tighter range within which the stock's suggested volatility generally lives. When selecting an underlying to trade, it is an expectation that a stock's implied volatility will return to this tight range over time that we can rely on. When we talk about indicated volatility being a mean going back function, this is exactly what we mean.

How can we use this in our trading? If we recall in time and prevent- my own a "regular," a high, and a low expectation for a stock's implied volatility, we can determine where in this range the current meant volatility lives. There are two ways that traders do this. The very first is to identify where the present implied volatility is as compared to its range for the time frame in which we are looking. So the computation would appear like this:

IV Range (or IV Rank) = (IV Current − IV Low)/(IV High − IV Low)

So, for example, if we are using a one-year time frame and the highest the implied volatility has been is 40, the lowest it has been is 20, and the current implied volatility is 25, the stocks IV percentile would be as follows:

$(25 - 20) / (40 - 20) = 5/20 = .25$, or 25th percentile

Some traders will mistakenly call this metric "IV Percentile." Mathematically, that is incorrect, and I will call this "IV Range." Although this calculation makes intuitive sense, it does not always reflect wherein its normal range the current implied volatility currently resides (and is, in fact, a ratio and not a percentile). To illustrate this, let's assume that the underlying represented earlier trades typically in the 20 to 25 IV range. Let's assume that in the past one year, or 252 trading days, the implied volatility for the underlying exceeded 25 in only one day. On this day, the implied volatility stood at 40 due to some unusual event. If today the implied volatility of this underlying stands at 25, the other calculation shows it to be in its 25th percentile. Yet it surely is trading at a reasonably costly implied volatility for the underlying as on all, but one day the implied volatility was less than or equal to its current reading. And this defines the second means of calculating the implied volatility percentile. Again assuming we are using one year, we can take the current implied volatility and determine how many days the implied volatility has exceeded or been beneath the current reading. Using this calculation, our implied volatility percentile for the other stock would be 99 percent or 100 percent, as the 25 percent IV was exceeded only once in the past year out of 252 reading days. While these two calculations do not always show such a dramatic difference, it is essential to take note of the strengths and weaknesses of each, as some software packages you will encounter may use one or the other of the calculations.

So how do we use this number in our trading? It would seem logical that if the underlying was trading at more magnificent than its 50th percentile, we might be interested in selling premium. And if the underlying was trading at less than its50th percentile, we might be interested in buying premium. After all, if we believe that implied volatility is mean reverting, doesn't that mean we believe the implied volatility will trend back toward its 50th percentile? In practicality, it is not that simple for three reasons.

First, as we have discussed, our option trades have a limited life span. So though I believe in mean reversion for implied volatility, It shouldn't be assumed that an option will complete its mean reversion before the option's expiration.

Secondly, when the market gets quiet and realized volatility slows, most underlying will fall to below their 50th percentile. It is often the case that during those times, the selling option premium gives us the best edge (the most extensive margin) between implied volatility and realized volatility. And unlike periods of high implied volatility in the general market, these quiet periods tend to last for long periods. They often last for over one year and have been known to last for as long as two years. If we traded underlying only when their implied volatility percentile was higher than the 50th percentile, we would have very little to do during these quiet periods. We would be missing out on money-making opportunities.

Lastly, underlying that are trading high in their IV percentile are often trading that way for a reason. Perhaps the stock has earnings coming up or some other type of announcement. Or maybe the stock's volatility has increased for another reason, such as the stock breaking out to new all-time highs or falling below its 52-week low, or simply because the industry the stock's business falls within has come upon hard times. Whatever the reason, recognition of the "event" and its timing will help you to make more informed trading decisions.

Rather than keying all your trades off that 50th implied volatility percentile, it is advisable to often compare an underlying's implied volatility percentile to that of the overall market. You will generally use either the SPX or the SPY as the representation of the global market. In general, you want an individual equity's IV percentile to be at least 15 percent higher than that of the overall market. That is required because a personal investment is subject to what I call "binary moves," whereas the SPX, as a diversified portfolio of stocks, is not nearly as affected by such events. It is also required that the IV percentile of the individual stock by over 35 percent. In this way, if the stock does mean revert in a short time frame, you do not get hurt too much by the volatility move. And this allows you to still build a short premium portfolio during the extended, low volatility environments we experience.

This implied volatility percentile, or implied volatility rank if that is all you have to work with, is the first thing you look at when trying to find an underlying you wish to trade. It allows you to compare underlying' implied volatilities on a relative basis, one against the other, and choose the underlying whose implied volatility is particularly high or unusually low for itself.

Having an underlying trading high in its range does not guarantee you will find a trade that you like, but from experience, this is the best place to start looking. So, begin your search with the underlying having the highest IV rank and continue through your watch list until you get to the name whose IV rank is 15 percent higher than that of the SPX. All of those underlying are potential premium-selling candidates.

Continuing our discussion of how to choose an underlying, let's assume we found XYZ stock to be high enough in its IV percentile to warrant further research. What do we do next? The first question that comes to mind is, "Why is XYZ stock trading with such a (relatively) high implied volatility?" So we do a little research. The first thing to check is when earnings are due out. We will spend time later discussing earnings in detail. As profits approach a stock's implied volatility, the percentile will appear high as it builds in other IV for the potential binary move to come. If you find XYZ will be reporting earnings within the next two weeks, you will move on to the following underlying in your list. During earnings season, this can get a bit tedious and frustrating, as most stocks that are high in their implied volatility percentile are top due to upcoming earnings. It is beneficial if your broker's trading platform in some way flags those stocks whose earnings dates are approaching, as mine does. But if revenues are not approaching and XYZ's implied volatility is high for other reasons, we need to continue our search.

Though we already know that one-year implied volatility percentile is high in its range, as that is the reason we got this far in our research, to begin with, the additional time frames add color to the picture. For example, if 11 months ago, some news came out on this particular stock that caused a great deal of price fluctuation, and the implied volatility rose for45 days, a 9-month picture would exclude that event. I may consider the past nine months as a more typical picture for the stock, or I may not, but at least I have that choice when I look at multiple time frames.

We now turn our attention to the term historical volatility, or realized volatility as it is sometimes called. Unlike implied volatility, which is a measure of future stock movement as predicted by (or built into) an option's price, historical volatility has nothing to do with options. It is not a predictor of future stock movement at all, but rather it is a reporter of past stock movement. The industry norm, if you will, is the 20-day (or 21-day) historical volatility of a stock's movement. Though I find historical volatility to be a useful indicator, at times, its value can be deceptive. To understand this, we need to review how historical volatility is calculated once again. Historical volatility is the standard deviation of an asset's returns over a past period of time. If the stock closes at the same price every day for 20 days, its historical volatility is zero. If the stock rises (or falls) 10 percent every day for 20 days, its historical volatility is also zero. So a stock that is trending steeply will have an historical volatility that is lower than one might expect. Thus, you should always be careful to review the stock chart to ensure you understand the stock's past behavior. If the stock is trending steeply, you discount the value of the historical volatility calculation.

Now let's assume that the historical volatility calculation seems to show the past behavior of the stock fairly. What good is it to our trading process? Many traders will say it has no value. They will say, "You have seen the disclaimer that past performance may not be indicative of future performance, have you not? In the same manner, looking at past stock performance has little bearing on future stock performance, and therefore, the historical volatility tells us nothing." Though I understand their point, I disagree. Indeed, past performance has some predictive value, or why would we prefer to sell KO implied volatility at 25 before we would sell FSLR implied volatility at 32?

For this reason, many traders simply look for a significant difference between an option's implied volatility and its underlying's historical volatility when lining up trades. Though I find this information to be useful, you need to remember that historical volatility is calculated using only 20 days of data and can, therefore, change quickly. What is found to be even more meaningful is the trend in the historical volatility.

Many traders will debate whether historical volatility leads to implied volatility or whether implied volatility leads to historical volatility. I often see historical volatility lead on the way up, and implied volatility lead on the way down. But before I change the nature of my portfolio, I like to see historical volatility trends going in one direction or the other. After all, the historical volatility calculation requires 5, 10, or 20 days of data, whereas the implied volatility is a snapshot in time and can whip back and forth much quicker.

Making an Assumption

An assumption of some kind drives every trade. It might be a directional assumption or implied volatility-related. Though most of my trades are driven by volatility assumptions (after all, that is the "edge" option most readily provide), most traders will be driven by directional hypotheses when making trades. This is true of technical analysts, fundamental analysts, contrarian traders, and your average investor. And this kind of directional trading can be done with virtually any instrument, options included. The advantage of directional options trading is the leverage you receive. The disadvantage, unless you are trading deep in the money options, is that to obtain an unlimited upside for your trade, you must purchase options (as opposed to selling them). As earlier discussed, when you are buying an option, you are paying more than the option is currently intrinsically worth. So your underlying must move a certain amount in your favor just for you to break even on the trade. If you are trading stocks or futures, this is not true. So purchasing options for a purely directional trade is akin to running the first 20 meters of a 100-meter dash in sand.

When you execute a directional trade by selling options, you have a limited profit potential with the possibility of unlimited losses. Of course, you gain the advantage of selling extrinsic value, and thus the underlying can actually move against you a bit, and you still make money. As such, you put the odds in your favor as a premium seller. But as you can see, this discussion has quickly moved away from using options as a directional vehicle to using options as a strategic vehicle. And that is as it should be. I will leave others to spend hundreds of millions of dollars trying to find a way to continually predict market direction more accurately than "Brownian motion with an upward drift" would predict. However, the bulk of your decision-making process, your trade assumption if you will, is not based on a directional assumption but a volatility assumption. This is the beauty of options trading. You can be as bad at choosing a stock's direction and still be highly profitable. Volatility assumptions are much easier to make, leave more room for error, and have a tendency for mean reversion that can guide you on your way. None of these things can be said of directional assumptions.

Each trader is different. There is a well-known trading psychologist by the name of Dr. Van Tharp, who begins each one of his newsletters with the statement, "I always say that people do not trade the markets; they trade their beliefs about the markets." I agree with Dr. Tharp, 100 percent. You may be thinking, "If every person reading this book is trading his or her own beliefs, and they differ considerably, how can we all be profitable? Isn't it the market that pays us?" This is to my point. It is your strategy and not the assumptions that can make you a consistently profitable trader. If you believe that statement, doesn't it make more sense to spend your time and money choosing and refining a strategy that can continuously grow your account, instead of wasting your time and money trying to predict the direction of a stock or the market in general? For me, the answer is a resounding yes.

Though the trade might begin with an assumption that may or may not be correct, it will always be supported by a volatility assumption, a proper choice of strategy, and a mathematically supported, positive expectancy exit strategy. And this is the crux of trading success, in my opinion.

Fundamental analysis holds excellent merit, in my opinion. If a company is growing at a long-term growth rate of 17 percent and its stock is trading at a 12 P/E, I find that pretty attractive. Based on those numbers, you might scoop up some stock, or you might sell some puts below the market in hopes of either capturing that premium or buying stock lower than it is trading. Those are rational actions to take based on the information given. But to assume the stock price will move up in the next 30 to 50 days is overreaching the limits of what fundamental analysis can do for you. The current price of the stock, in an efficient market, theoretically takes into account all known information. To assume that the marketplace is mispricing a company so dramatically that you think the stock will move considerably in the next 30 to 50 days is a fool's errand, in my opinion. So, though I believe in the validity of fundamental analysis, I think it has little application in the short time frame world in which my options trading resides. In other words, it is a timing issue and not a problem with the analysis itself.

The third means of arriving at a directional assumption is what we term contrarian trading. Contrarian traders generally take the other side of extended moves in a stock or in the overall market itself. They try to take advantage of markets that are overdone on either side. When a stock catches fire, so to speak, and runs up very far, very fast, a contrarian trader will often step in and get short that stock, hoping for a turnaround in its price. As I said, the same is right on the downside. When they feel the "baby has been thrown out with the bathwater," and the stock has taken more abuse than is warranted, they will be there to get long the stock. It has been observed that many contrarians have a decent track record when measured by the percentage of time they are correct. Unfortunately, when measured by their profitability, they seem to have less success. Intuitively those statements don't seem to go together. But thinking about the nature of those stocks, we can make some sense of it. A stock that has run up very far, very fast, is what we term "in play." It has acquired significant velocity, and the farther up it runs, the more speed it seems to pick up. We used to term getting in front of these moves, "picking up nickels in front of a steamroller." In other words, when you are wrong, you are dead wrong. Due to the velocity of the stock at the time the contrarian steps in, when one is wrong, the losses can be brutal.

The primary point to note here is that unless you can predict stock movement in a time frame that matches your trades' timing, spending a lot of time and money trying is wasted effort. And even if you believe you can learn to predict the direction and magnitude of short-term moves, I still think option strategy is easier to learn and provides a better outcome.

.

CHAPTER NINE

ExitingTrades

Majority of traders exit by "fear" rather than by mechanics. They stubbornly refuse to take a loss and think that makes them much better traders in the end. As a person who believes strongly in the power of mathematics, I would like to change that. We will discuss what an appropriate mechanical strategy looks like and how to create one. We will likewise take a look at when it is allowed to deviate from the plan and when it is crucial not to depart. This will happen in the context of a method with a favorable span. We will examine the three situations that lead us to exit the trade and dissect what each suggests to our probability presumptions.

•The Variables

What variables must we resolve for (or a minimum of comprehend) to produce a positive expectancy trading method? It sounds like a challenging question; it has an easy answer. Even the traders who work by gut feel have an understanding that the "edge vs. odds" relationship is essential to success. In other words, the higher the chances of success or the more significant the edge in the trade, the bigger the threat you should take on with the business. What is essential to take away from this explanation is that there are three carefully linked inputs to the decision. They are the possibility of winning, the average benefit when you gain, and the average expense when you lose. These are "3 legs of the stool" that make up your strategy, and all three are inexplicably linked. When someone asks me, "When should I take my losses?" it is difficult to respond to that without the context of when they are taking their earnings and how regularly they are benefiting and losing.

You may be questioning if you will ever have the ability to understand how to develop a winning technique with all these interconnected pieces complicating the issue. How are they interconnected? How will I know if my method has a definite span? Thankfully, there was a researcher by the name of John Kelly operating at Bell Labs who, back in 1956, obtained a formula to help in a sound reduction for long-distance calls. People rapidly realized Kelly's method (or Kelly's Criterion, as it is typically called) had applications for gambling and position sizing in trading. Let's analyze this little gem and see what we can discover.

The Kelly Criterion

As we discussed, the Kelly Criterion can help us stabilize the three legs of the stool connected with our trading technique. The simplified formula, used for position sizing, looks like this:

Kelly percent = W − [(1 − W)/ R]

Where;

W = portion of winners (or if forecasting, probability of revenue).

R = average gain of our winning trades/average loss of our losing trades.

How do we use this formula for position sizing to assist in building our technique? Let's begin by taking a look at where Kelly percent is equivalent to zero. This would indicate the method is neither for a loser nor a winner; however, instead is a breakeven. We can "back off" one of the three variables to produce a winning formula.

Replacing 0 for Kelly percent, we can streamline our formula as follows:

0 = W − [1 − W/ R] R = (1/W) − 1.

W =1/(R +1).

These identify the break-even relationships between our three variables. Given any two of the variables, you can figure out the break-even value from the 3rd. Let's look at a few examples. In these examples, we will presume we have made short premium trades and that the overall credit gotten on each trade will be represented by 100 percent. If we offer a strangle for $4 and we let it end useless, we make 100 percent. We have a 75 percent earnings ($ 4-- $1)/$ 4 =.75 (or 75%) if we purchase it back for $1.

To Log Your Trades or Not to Log Your Trades

Typically a topic of intense debate is whether it is worth the time and effort to log your trades. You will remember your genuinely painful businesses without the requirement to compose them down. And if you make a note of the right trades, this may keep you from successfully embellishing the stories over cocktails at a later date and time. So, why trouble with all the small trades or trades that had little impact on your account? As I hope you keep in mind by now, alternatives trading is a probability-based activity. Here are a couple of reasons you need to keep a detailed trading log and a couple of methods you need to use your diary to guide you as you progress.

1. Though the option chain anticipates your possibility of earnings for you, there is no guarantee that your outcomes will match them precisely. If you collect your trading data for an extended amount of time and discover that your real percentage of trades that pay does not match what the option chain

anticipated, you have a flaw in the method you are picking either your underlying or your trades. However, it is generally the option of underlying that triggers the possibilities to veer off the predicted path, from my experience. Going back through those areas of this book that cover "picking your underlying" or "picking a strategy" needs to help you in determining where you are going incorrect. If not, you may need a session with an excellent choices coach to point you in the right direction. The excellent news is that for any decent alternatives coach, this is usually a quick fix.

2. A "three-legged stool" that helps us produce a trading strategy that has a favorable span (i.e., it specifies a rewarding trading methodology). And among the three legs is our likelihood of revenue. Without this piece, we can not determine the appropriate levels to close our trades, both on the earnings side and the losing side. Using the probabilities from the option chain is an excellent place to begin. Over time, if we study our logs and the data that come out of it, we can get better possibilities to guide us in our exit levels. Traders who are against keeping a diary are usually not using any kind of exit strategy based upon probabilities. If they are and are not logging their trades, they are trading so infrequently that they can track them in their heads. And that is an entirely various problem, as you require a sensible variety of occurrences for the possibilities to work. Back to my point: If you do not log your trades, it is

challenging to abide and remember by your Kelly Criterion exit methods.

3. Though this may appear silly, I discover that without logging trades, it is a lot more difficult for a new trader to think the discipline of trading is as simple and as necessary as I discover it to be. And when that holds, it is a lot easier for a trader to drift off strategy. So, a trade log can hammer house the point that trading is indeed a "discipline." Checking out six or nine months of trades and seeing that your trade likelihoods are within a couple of percent of what was forecasted by the choice chain can be an eye-opening workout for newer traders, and even for knowledgeable traders. They try logging their trades for the very first time.

4. This is a close analogy to number one; a log is the simplest way of discovering errors in your method. Patterns you might not anticipate to see will frequently pop out of a cautious evaluation of your record.

So, what type of info is beneficial in a trading log? The more information you select to log, the more of your time the registration uses up. And since time is money, it makes good sense to attempt to keep this data collection to a minimum. But no one ever stated trading did not require some effort. The beautiful part of creating a trading log is that it can be occupied after trading hours or after work hours. Though a few numbers may alter throughout the day, you can easily either re-create or insert those numbers in the evening or on the weekend. Of course, the closer to the trade time you log the trade, the more comfortable and more accurate it will be. And the more details you gather, the better the log will be to your trading. So, this is a place I would not skimp. I would collect all the details you feel you may require. It is far simpler to gather it in advance than to attempt to go back in time and re-create the numbers.

When keeping your log, bear in mind that the primary purpose is to be able to compare expected probabilities to actual likelihoods over a prolonged duration of time. As such, you will be logging information from when you made the trade and expectations from the profession, as well as recording your exits and the actual probabilities you incur.

Here are a couple of fields I discover work for a trade log and how they can be made use of.

1. Trade entry date: I always log the year I made the trade. This will work in a couple of ways, which we will detail later.

2. The sign of the underlying traded: As we discussed previously, when we do our "trade forensics" after a minimum of several months of data are gathered, among the things we look for are symbols that regularly do not carry out as their alternative chain predicts. Hence, we need to be able to sort by the logo in our spreadsheet to accumulate this information quickly.

3. The trading strategy employed: Not only do I like to see how my strangles, my iron condors, and my long straddles are doing. However, I also want to code whether my trades are undefined or specified threat techniques. I can then see how my probabilities are tracking expected results on a number of various levels.

4. The rate of the underlying at the time of the trade: This enables one to see the magnitude of the relocation in the underlying from trade entry to trade exit. You might begin logging your trades (or begin trading, for that matter) right at the start of some high historical volatility. If that is so, these numbers will assist you to figure out.

5. The strikes traded: This is handy when managing your trades, but can end up being a tough thing to track if you roll your sell any manner. There are a plethora of methods to follow this if you do run a trade. Analyze the best way to set up your own log.

6. The variety of agreements traded: This is crucial in tracking your success and to recall to ensure you are sizing your trades correctly. If your probabilities are following well, however, you are not making cash sizing is the most common cause—more on this during our section on portfolio management.

7. The possibility of earnings as defined by your option chain: This is an essential piece of information for the way we use our logs. Remember that this is not the likelihood of ending up out

of the cash, but rather the possibility of breakeven. With brief premium techniques, the probability of breakeven will be higher than the likelihood of expiring out of the money.

8. The implied volatility at the time of the trade: This can be tracked in a number of ways. You can either keep the implied volatility of the at the cash option for the expiration cycle you are trading or keep the implied volatility of each strike you trade. The latter offers far more details; for the starting trader, I discover the information to be extreme. The extra data can be used in discerning alter and other changes in the distribution curve. But determining that information is hard. I discover keeping the at the cash implied volatility is enough.

9. The premium invested or got throughout the trade: Having the net rate of the business is very vital if you are going to use the spreadsheet to track your trade exits as specified by your Kelly Criterion. It is likewise required if you are following your earnings and loss details.

10. I like to set up my log so that I either input the portion of max profit at which I wish to take my earnings and the edge I want from the anticipated likelihood (typically in between 10 and 15 percent) or input both the portion of max profit at which I want to take my earnings and my piece at which I want to take my loss. In either case, I compute the costs, both profits and loss, at which I desire to leave my trade. Whichever price the trade strikes first is my exit point. By having this calculated at

the time I enter the trade into my log, I know instantly where my exit points are. And by having them in my log, I can describe them at any time.

11. Specific pieces of info on the exit: The very first piece of information is the date we make the exit trade. From that date, we can determine and log the number of days we were in our trade.

12. The rate at which you close your trade: From this information, you can determine your actual possibility of earnings for comparison with what the choice chain anticipated. You can also identify your profits or loss for the trade.

13. Some other fields: We can determine profits and losses, number and portions of winners and losers, and percentage differences from anticipated. We can break these fields down by classifications, like defined risk trades versus undefined risk trades, or by particular trading methods, like strangles or iron condors. We can find out how we are doing with our long premium trades versus our short premium trades. We can see if we work with our profits trades. We can find underlying that are carrying out well or performing inadequately. The kind of information you can pull from your log is limited just by your creativity.

As you can observe, a trade log is a beneficial tool for helping fine-tune and track our trading techniques. I use Excel for producing my log, however a few of the traders I coach use Google Docs spreadsheets, FileMaker Pro, or other shows languages to track their trades. So, it can be an elementary program or a more complicated means of accumulating the information. Start basic and grow your log as you please. The goal is to get the very best return for your time. Once you begin logging your trades and pulling info out of it, it becomes quite addicting. It is a vital tool to assist you in your trading.

CHAPTER TEN

Portfolio Management

We have discussed how to choose individual trades, how to best exit your trades, and when to exit trades both as winners and losers. Once you have many trades on your sheets, what should you do to manage your overall portfolio's danger? How do you know what the total threat is?

We will start our conversation by exploring a more academic viewpoint on the concern and continue to a more practical method. I need to warn you that for each educator you check out or listen to, you will more than likely get different answers regarding the very best method to control your risk.

What I will provide to you is a solid structure for how to see your threat, some possible trade concepts to help reduce the portfolio's risk, and some general rules as to how to size your trades. You may be questioning why sizing your trades appears in a portfolio management conversation.

Two Types of Risk

Many people hear the term threat and believe it refers to how much they can lose. That is not wrong; there is much more to the story. And knowing a few more of the information will help you much better comprehend the nature of your portfolio.

People, by nature, are risk-averse. The majority of us would choose not to take any danger, all else being equal. There are those couple of risk-takers out there who take on risk solely for the sake to rush opportunities. I would extremely recommend those individuals to stay away from trading. They will get their rush and then the call from their broker, letting them know their account is closed due to a lack of funds. Every trade is a moving danger. By lining up trades where the implied volatility exceeds its norm and its historical volatility, we feel appropriately compensated in the majority of circumstances. But we need to comprehend a bit more about the risk to handle it properly. There are two types of risks of which every trader should understand.

• Unique Risk

The very first type of danger is a unique risk. This refers to risk specific to a company or a stock. They consist of management changes, quality of management, company profits surprises, lawsuits, bad press, and getting outcompeted, among others. When thinking about distinct risks, imagine an event that will affect just one company or a small circle of associated companies. This risk can likewise be broadened to a market, though the market threat is a little a hybrid. The point you need to be familiar with is that distinct risk can be diversified to restrict the quantity of danger new trades may contribute to the portfolio.

- Systematic Risk

The second type of risk is systematic; this refers to macro-level threats, such as that provided by political events or large financial policy occasions. Examples may be war breaking out, oil prices increasing, a surprise rate trek, or health issues of a high-ranking authorities in the federal government or Federal Reserve. These occasions impact essentially on trades. This is the kind of danger that can not be diversified away, frequently comes unexpectedly, and need to be mitigated, in the majority of circumstances. Your portfolio ought to preserve some type of balance concerning direction, property, industry, and volatility class. That is not to say you must be perfectly balanced. It simply means you need to be familiar with the level of systematic risk your portfolio carries and guarantee you feel you are getting adequate threat premiums for the level of danger you bring.

The Goal: Diversification of Minimizing Unique Risk

At this point, we will look in more depth at the theory behind the diversification of special threats. First, as options traders, we are noticeably knowledgeable about suggested volatility as a threat in every trade we make. And, as we have discussed, implied volatility is nothing more than the basic discrepancy of the distribution curve of our underlying's movement. Each specific underlying has its own, distinct standard difference. In modern monetary management courses, we use that basic discrepancy as a measure of threat in a business. We can recall over a minimum of a 60-month (5-year) duration and identify what that basic deviation is? Any statistics book can assist you with this if you are not knowledgeable about how to compute it. You can use a spreadsheet, like Excel, and use its built-in standard deviation function to show up at a solution. We can also calculate the fundamental discrepancy for a varied portfolio, such as the S&P 500 (as represented by the SPX). I have selected to compute the standard discrepancy for twelve securities for a 20-year duration to help in our conversation. These 12 securities consist of 11 members of the SPX, and the SPX itself. See the next table for the information.

Looking at this data, we see a wide variety of necessary deviations, and therefore risk, amongst our underlying. The one thing that must stand out is that the diversified portfolio of stocks, the SPX, has the lowest step of risk. If we were to take all 500 securities, determine their essential variance, and average (weighted or not), the typical basic variation would be far more significant than the basic discrepancy of the SPX. In reality, that is not diversification works. Diversity is the phenomenon where the typical basic disparity of the parts of a portfolio is much greater than the standard discrepancy of the combined portfolio. Why is this? It is because the distinct threats are canceling each other out! One caution to be familiar with is the underlying in your portfolio needs to be diverse. That means they should be reasonably uncorrelated or inversely correlated. If you are trading two related securities, the distinct risks will not cancel.

Option Trading Software - Why You Should Never Analyze Option Stocks Manually

Whether you are an experienced trader or anew comer in the field of stock trading, using Option Trading Software to trade will significantly boost your capability to trade correctly in the stock market.

If you are searching for an automated software application to trade with, then you ought to have been familiar with the term options trading.

This section of the book will teach you the essentials of options and what to look for when searching for automated software, especially the ones that are used for trading options. Why trouble trading manually, trying to find out complicated stock analysis, when there are software application packages readily available to fix this.

Options are contracts or financial contracts that are comparable to stocks. In truth, they can be traded similar to stocks. Options offer various trading solutions for traders that are more open to new ways to trade efficiently in public markets.

Options can, at times, be perilous, and even the smart investor can lose cash on a wrong trade choice, without evaluating the opportunity rapidly. Stock options are time delicate and will end quickly. Quick analyses of options are required to be effective.

Options end extremely rapidly at times, dramatically affecting the cost of the choice. That is why using option trading software to examine robust and complex factors of the marketplace quickly, is vital to a trader's success. Stock values can alter quickly at times, and using manual methods to trade will trigger you to be at a downside.

Options trading software application will correctly select the ideal stocks for you. You can materialize money fast if you use options trading software application, but you should remember that the software is not totally automated. Human intervention is required at times. The important point that you ought to remember is not to completely depend on automated software applications to do the work for you, but using trading software will give you the very best chances for success.

Although automated trading software application is used for trading stocks, you need to learn and understand how it is done, in the event you need to do it by hand. There are free and paid software applications offered for use, but paid ones will have more alternatives available.

Options trading software application is available as online services, or software that is installed straight on your computer. Both have advantages and disadvantages. Software application set up on your computer will probably not require a month-to-month subscription charge for use because you would be using your own computer system resources. All you have to be sure of is that the software application vendor uses totally free updates and upgrades to your set up the software application.

Using online alternative trading software application affords you the chance of not having to fret about updates to the software application. The creator of the software application will look after all updates and upgrades, given that you will be using the software application from their computers. The only disadvantage may be the continuous regular monthly membership fee.

Another advantage of using alternative trading software as an online service is that your trade history will be conserved and instantly backed up by the owner of the software application. If you use the software set up on your computer system and your computer system crashes, you may lose information if not doing a day-to-day backup.

Manual trading is excellent, however, using options trading Software is better. Why waste valuable time by manually trying to find out the complexities of discovering exceptional Option Stocks.

CHAPTER ELEVEN

why do You TradeWeekly Options?

Weekly options have remained in existence for long, but in numerous stocks, a week represents over 30 percent of the total option volume. The development is still exponential, and that has brought liquidity and a fantastic chance. I have been an options trader for years, and more than 95 percent of my income has come as a direct outcome of trading stock choices and futures choices. In those years, I have never seen an item with the potential to offer the typical investor a possibility to compete on relatively equivalent footing with the expert traders.

Trading choices, stock, and futures are all zero-sum video games. Simply stated, when I offer or purchase something in an auction market, I must find a buyer or seller who is ready to do the opposite side of the trade. In the end, among us will win what the other loses. If I make this trade to infinity, both of us will have the very same P & L, minus commissions. Because our capital is not infinite and commissions are, both people will ultimately wind up broke.

When you are thinking about making trading your profession, that is a critical note! Let's go back to a game of possibility once again-poker. You enter a game with nine other players. Each of you needs to invest $100, and you must play the video game to the end of each hand. The home" rakes" (commission) $1 per hand. How long does the game last? In this circumstance, the game would last around 1,000 hands. At that point, the home would have taken all the players' money in the form of commission. This is a zero-sum video game plus commissions, extremely much the like trading alternatives.

I discussed what makes a possession tradable. The first thing that I require is that it is liquid. I define liquidity as the ability to get in and exit a property effortlessly to the possible gain. If our possible benefit, usually, is $100, but the quote offer spread is $10, that asset is not liquid. It will cost us $10 to enter and $10 to exit, and if our commission is $10, we are giving up a 30 percent edge to our possible gain. On any private trade, you might generate income, but in the long run, no matter how excellent you are, you will lose. On the other hand, if our quote-- use spread is just $1 and our commission is $1.00, is it possible to conquer the edge and turn a profit gradually?

I have now developed what it takes to conquer the zero-sum choice market. You need to have a combination of fast quote-- provide spreads, low commission, and more ability than your opponent.

Weekly alternatives are a little variation of the longer-term serials, but that is where the resemblance ends.

CHAPTER TWELVE

Traits of a Successful Options Trader

Regardless of its numerous benefits, options trading brings considerable risk of loss, and it is extremely speculative. Like any other business, being a successful options trader requires a certain capability, character type, and attitude.

1. Be Able to Manage Risk

Options are high-risk instruments, and it is necessary for traders to acknowledge how much danger they have at any point in time. What is the optimum downside of the trade? What is the specific or implicit position with regard to volatility? Just how much of my capital is designated to the trade? These are some of the concerns traders always have to keep in their minds.

Traders likewise require to take proper procedures to manage risk. If you are a committed short-term options trader, you will frequently stumble upon loss-making trades. You need to be able to reduce the risk of your positions at any time. Some traders do so by restricting their trade size and diversifying into several trades, so all their eggs aren't in the exact same basket.

An options trader also needs to be an excellent money supervisor. They require to utilize their capital wisely. It would not be wise to obstruct 90% of your capital in a single trade. Whatever technique you adopt, risk management and cash management can not be disregarded.

2. Be Excellent With Numbers

In the course of trading in options, you are always dealing with numbers. What is volatility? What's the break-even of the trade? Options traders are always answering these questions. They likewise refer to option Greeks, such as the delta, gamma, vega, and theta of their options trades.

3. Have Discipline.

To become successful, options traders need to practice discipline. Doing a comprehensive research study, recognizing changes, setting up the best trade, sticking and forming to a technique, setting up goals, and developing an exit method are all part of the discipline. An easy example of deviating from the training is following the herd. Never rely on an opinion without doing your research study. Instead, you need to devise an independent trading method that operates for it to be an effective options strategy.

While formal education in the kind of higher degrees can be related to elite traders, it is not always the case for all. You must be informed about the market. Active traders take some time to find out the basics and study the marketplace-- numerous scenarios, different trends-- anything and everything about how the market works. They are not normally newbies who have taken a three-hour trading seminar on "How to get rich quick trading," however rather make an effort to discover from the marketplace.

4. Be Patient.

Client investors are willing to await the marketplace to offer the best chance instead of attempting to make a big win on every market movement. The very same is not the case with amateur traders. They are restless, unable to control their feelings, and they will be quick to go into and exit trades.

5. Establish a Trading Style.

Each trader has various personalities and needs to embrace a trading style that fits his or her characteristics. Some traders might be good at day trading, where they purchase and sell options several times during the day to make small earnings. Some may be comfier with position trading, where they form trading methods to benefit from distinct opportunities, such as volatility and time decay. And others can be more comfortable with swing trading, where traders make bets on rate movement over durations lasting five to 30 days.

6. Analyze the News.

It is vital for traders to be able to analyze the news, different hype from truth, and make suitable decisions based upon this understanding. You will discover numerous traders excited to put their capital in an option with promising news, and the next day they will proceed to the next huge story. This distracts them from recognizing larger patterns in the market. A lot of effective traders will be truthful with themselves and make sound personal options, instead of just passing the significant stories in the news.

7. Be an Active Learner.

The Chicago Board of Trade (CBOT) reported 90% of options traders would understand losses. What separates successful traders from typical ones succeeds traders are able to gain from their losses and execute what they find out in their trading methods. Elite traders practice until they discover the lessons behind the trade, and see the market behavior as it is taking place.

The monetary markets are constantly changing and developing; you need to have a clear understanding of what's taking place and how all of it works. By ending up being an active learner, you will not only become great at your current trading techniques, but however, you will also be able to recognize new opportunities others may not see or might pass over.

8. Be Flexible.

You can not stake a claim on the marketplace but should opt for the market or get out of it when it is not the type that fits you. You need to accept losses take place which it is inevitable that you will lose. Acceptance rather than battling the market is vital to understanding, clarity, and finally winning.

9. Strategy Your Trades.

An options trader who prepares is most likely to be successful than the trader who operates on instinct and feel. If you don't have a plan, you will place random trades, and consequently, you'll be directionless. On the other hand, if you have a plan, you are more likely to stay with it. You should be very clear about what your goals are and how you plan to attain them. When to book profits, you will also understand how to cover your losses or. You can see how the plan has actually worked (or not worked) for you. All these steps are important to establishing a strong trading strategy.

10. Keep Records.

A lot of effective options traders keep persistent records of their trades. Maintaining proper trade records is an important habit to assist you to avoid making costly decisions. The history of your trade records likewise supplies a wealth of info to assist you enhance your odds of success.

The Bottom Line.

Top options traders get joy from scouting and enjoying their trades. Sure, it's excellent to see an option come out on top, however, just like sports fans, options traders delight in viewing the entire game unfold, not just discovering out the last score. These attributes will not guarantee your success in the options trading world, but they will definitely increase your chances at it.

The Psychological Component to Options Trading

Being successful with options is not always the simplest thing to attain. Sure, there are some that have made a great success in their endeavors into the world of options trading. These individuals are among those that lots of will look towards as motivation for their options trading adventures. There will be those that will look towards these success stories for more than motivation. They will look towards effective options traders as those to replicate. Or, more properly, they will attempt to replicate the trading techniques and techniques of the trader.

While it is definitely a wise thing to look towards the trading methods of an effective trader, replicating the actions of the trader alone might not prove to be the best technique. The reason for this is that there are other factors that go into the process of establishing a trading method than simply the execution of the trades. Individual aspects will enter into the development of an approach. In some circumstances, there will be mental factors that will be turned into the trading strategies. Understanding such parts is essential to exploring a trading approach to make sure it is critical to your goals.

It would not harm you to explore your psychological aspects and elements before seriously at trading. Now, some might presume such assessments are little more than 'psycho-babble' that look at options trading from an over-analytical perspective. This might be the case in some instances, but as a general description of what inspires people towards options trading, it is not something you want to overlook. By having a clear understanding of your mental makeup, you can develop the appropriate insight into how to be efficient in the art of trading.

Some people are more cut out for options trading than others. Those that are conservative in their investment techniques may want to restrict options trading to a smaller sized part of their general portfolio. Those that can be thought about rather aggressive in their method might look towards possibly using options as a hedge to their portfolio. Again, your own personal psychological makeup regarding comfort levels of trading in important in options. This will definitely help promote your capability to find the correct response to whether you are cut out for options trading.

How can you discover whether you have the frame of mind of an options trader? The initial step includes truthfully answering whether you are somebody that possesses the discipline to be an options trader. Some might believe they have the discipline to succeed. Thinking you possess specific attributes to a specific degree and, in fact, having those attributes to the proper degree are two completely various things. Understanding exactly where you stand in regards to your mindset and your levels of discipline will help in improving your chances of success.

Somebody who requires to keep fiddling with their account by purchasing and offering every few days isn't somebody who should be investing in options! The commissions alone will eat you up. Someone who likes a lot of excitement in their trading must probably remain away from options.

Having a quality options trading technique is handy. Putting the options trading strategy through to fruition is a lot more valuable. Then again, there is a big difference in having the desire to follow such a procedure and actually following through with it. Those that have the ability to follow through with such steps may be limited in number. No, that is not stated as a method of weakening anyone's morale, motivation, or desire. Rather, it is a method of effectively forecasting the management of your endeavor and examining the danger of getting included with options trading. You also need a strategy for when the market goes against your method so that you do not make options due to the fact that you're panicking.

Yes, trading in options needs to be looked at from the point of view of managing a small company. When running a small company, you require to assess the risk connected with a venture. You also require to assess the capacities and dangers related to the success or failure of the business. This same ideology needs to be put towards options trading. If you can honestly assess yourself as someone with the self-discipline to follow through with a reliable options trading method, then you may extremely well be very successful with options trading.

How well can you handle losing trades? Are you able to manage losses and pick things up and begin the procedure over again? If you are, then you might effectively embody the proper psychological makeup for being successful with options trading. Those that can not handle the pressure of the periodic loss would be much better served looking towards another investing strategy.

It has actually been stated success begins with the ideal mental makeup. You might discover success is not as elusive as you believe if you can adjust your frame of mind to your psychological approach to trading.

CHAPTER THIRTEEN

SelectingaPortfolio trade

Finally, you have actually learned how to do lots of things trading weekly options. We have examined how markets are organized and how they buy, identified the numerous market participants, and how they shape the market results. The book has explained why it is necessary to continually sell liquid markets and how to recognize the qualities that constitute liquidity. The phases of the marketplace were identified, and a mathematical explanation was provided to describe how and why they rotate around the mean. The option model was dissected, and you were taught how to price it like an expert market maker. Easy trades were recommended that would permit you to effectively trade in any market conditions. Finally, the trades were wed to the marketplace conditions and the ones that work best when it is in any of the market stages.

All of the preliminary information is now in place, and it is time to discover how to arrange and trade a portfolio.

All of the technical work that has actually been done so far will not help you if you do not know how to arrange a portfolio of stocks. This is among the essential aspects of trading, due to the fact that your portfolio represents all of your liquid properties, cash! If you are not aware of where to invest your money, the possibilities of beating the market will go to absolutely no. The portfolio that you pick need to be in proportion to the amount of danger capital that you have to deal with; in addition, the diversification of the collection is essential.

The option procedure will be performed in 4 actions, and it is a screening procedure that is universal. By that, it indicates that the only thing that alters is the quantity of risk capital that you need to trade. The principles remain the exact same.

■ Liquidity

By now, you are most likely tired of finding out about liquidity; however, acknowledging liquidity in a portfolio is a little different than cash in a single trade.

When establishing a portfolio, the three aspects concerning liquidity are: the quote-- use spread, the expected series of the stock, and the size of the hidden security.

You will be trying to find stocks that are somewhere in between Priceline and Bank of America. There are hundreds of stocks that fit that mold, and they are constantly changing. Years ago, Facebook didn't exist as a public company, and now it is! Tight spreads, cost of over $50 a share, and excellent varieties. Look for stocks that are priced at $50 or higher or have a unique history of volatility.

■ Volatility

Liquidity was the first quality that we looked at; the 2nd characteristic is volatility. Volatility is the amount of air in the balloon in relation to the underlying stock cost. As an example, two stocks can be priced at $50. One is a utility that has been trading in a $5 variety for the past year. It is a dividend stock and is extremely stable. It is possible something could take place that would alter the price of the stock unexpectedly, but the opportunities are slim. The average anticipated variety for a weekly alternative would most likely remain in the $1 range.

This segment of the market has an excellent degree of unpredictability. The stock has actually more than quadrupled in price in the past year, and you would believe that it would have a much wider anticipated range; based upon history, you can be sure that the anticipated variety will be at least $4 and most likely more.

When we price a portfolio, in addition to liquidity, you need to consider volatility. If you are picking between 2 stocks with similar dollar rates, the more unpredictable stock is the one you desire in your portfolio.

If you are a financier, you like to have an extremely smooth trip in which you rarely trade in the marketplace; you don't care if you get a great deal of rate motion, you just desire long-lasting return. A trader needs a great deal of rate movement to offset the slippage that is lost in quote-- offer commissions and spreads.

■ Diversification by Product

Diversification by list is the next action in the procedure of establishing your portfolio. You want to ensure that the stocks that you are selecting are all not from the same group (duplication). This needs to be logical; you want to make sure that if one sector of the market is bullish, and another is bearish, you stabilize your portfolio in between the two segments.

As an example, if you choose that you desire to trade a financial stock, you can take a look at a variety of them and put the first two steps, liquidity and volatility, to the test. You then can decide from your technical indications which one appears to offer you the best possibility presently to cash a ticket. Place that stock in your portfolio and then go on to the next group. You are prepared to start trading when you have at least five stocks from various groups in place.

In addition to trading your portfolio, you need to watch extra stocks in the groupings to make sure that you are keeping your portfolio approximately date. If you are trading at the maximum portfolio size of $100,000+, you ought to be observed at least 50 stocks that fit the requirements of liquidity and volatility at all times. Even if you are trading at the minimum size of $1,000, you need at least ten stocks in your observation list.

■ Diversification by Dollar Risk

This is a fundamental principle and one that is frequently misused not just by first time traders, however by lots of veterans. Dollar diversification is used to offset the likelihood of risk.

Here is how it works.

We are back in the casino once again, playing blackjack. This time we are in your house, and there are two players against us. One is wagering $500 a hand, and one is betting $5 at hand. We understand the chances are somewhat in our favor, as we have the mathematical edge, so in the long run, we must anticipate the very same outcomes no matter which player wins. As a matter of truth, we enjoy seeing the enormous shooter, because, in theory, he must lose more to us in the long run. But here is where the problem comes in. Expect the vast shooter is an expert card counter, and the $5 gamer is having fun. The $5 player is there to take pleasure in the adventure. He is out the door; it does not have any impact on him if he loses his $50 bankroll. The $500 gamer is attempting to beat your home, and in the long run, possibly he suffices to do it. Given that the players are so out of balance, the casino could win its theoretical drop; however, lose money-- not an excellent scenario to be in.

If you do not account for the dollar distinction in your portfolio, this is the same problem that you will experience. The reason I used the $50 stocks earlier was to show you that diversification by rate and group is not enough. Suppose that your portfolio holds 100 shares of the $50 energy stock that has a typical weekly move of $1 and 100 shares of the $50 green energy stock that has an average variety of about $4. You must have the ability to see that you are not balanced; you would require to win four times as much in the energy stock on average to balance out one theoretical loss in the green stock, assuming the loss was understood at the expected relocation.

One might win 75 percent of your trades and still lose cash! An unbalanced dollar portfolio is more dangerous than one containing a lot of stocks of the same grouping. One hundred shares of Caterpillar are not like trading 100 shares of Netflix, and you need to accommodate this in order to balance your portfolio.

Balancing your portfolio is performed in steps:

Step one.

Take the stock with the highest Weekly EV and designate it a value of 1.

Step two.

Divide the EV of all other stocks buy the EV in the most significant stock.

Step three.

Trade the rest of step two and appoint it the correct number of contracts.

Consistently round to the nearest number of agreements; do not be concerned if your ratios are slightly off; unless you are trading hundreds of contracts, the rounding will have no result. The concept is to stabilize the dollars in the portfolio as close as you can to the current EV levels.

Handling money is the most crucial part of trading. If you wish to contend with expert traders, you need to know how they take a look at the marketplace. They are always trying to figure out a method to reduce their exposure. Unless it is a market-making function where they are your home, they are not going to get included in illiquid markets. They will trade a well-balanced portfolio, and you must likewise purchase one.

CHAPTER FOURTEEN

Stock Options Trading Newbie Mistakes

Error 1: Choosing the wrong options

Lots of options trading newbies choose to buy "cheap" options. Well, that person decision alone had resulted in much of the preliminary losses when a stock moved up insignificantly, and the position stays in a loss. Suppose you anticipate the stock to move powerfully in that instructions. Buying options of low amount of money also the reason that many options trading beginners lose all their money in one go. This takes place when the options they bought never turn into profit.

Error 2: Making complex positions as your first couple of tries at options trading

Many options trading newbies begin making sophisticated positioning strategies such as iron condor spread or butterfly spreads as their very first few options trades and then totally mess up as they did not understand how to keep the position and some don't even understand how to set up the positions correctly. When your trading experience is as detailed as they are, sophisticated techniques are just excellent.

Error 3: Buying options that do not conform to your expected trading horizon

The majority of options trading novices have no idea what an expected trading horizon is in the top place and typically find the options they purchase expiring before the underlying stock made the move they expected it to.

Error 4: Placing the wrong orders

Yes, when under pressure, specifically when real money is included, newbies tend to make silly human mistakes such as clicking an incorrect button, purchasing an incorrect option, purchasing an incorrect expiration month, or positioning a wrong stop-loss order that got the position sold right away. Such beginner human mistakes can only be lowered through an extended period of virtual trading practice on your selected options platform and, after that, gradually practice using only really little cash in order to get used to the sensation of trading genuine money. Unfortunately, we are all human, while skilled options traders tend to make lower of such mistakes, they still do often. It is more widespread in rookie trades and definitely injures trading self-confidence. Regularly give yourself a couple of months of virtual trading practice on your chosen platform before going on genuine cash.

Error 5: Trading with obtained money (or money you can not manage to lose).

There is a saying, "you can't pay to win if you can't manage to lose." This is incredibly true in trading, not just options trading, but any type of trading. If you trade using money that you can not pay for to lose, the mental pressure will minimize your odds of winning when your chances of winning are currently meager as a beginner. This is why we continuously encourage people to trade just with cash they can pay for to lose.

Error 6: Trading without assistance.

Would you discover to drive a car and truck without anyone guiding you? Why then would you try to trade without anybody guiding you? Yes, a teacher or a mentor is very crucial to a newbie in options trading not since they can provide you "tips" but because they can shed light on your scenario and reveal weak points that you might not have discovered. Newbies trading without assistance frequently repeat mistakes over and over again, and if you have traded option before, you know it don't take a lot of those mistakes to wipe your account out.

There you have, the leading six mistakes that newbies make in stock options trading. Take note of these frequently made mistakes, and you will prevent the disappointment of losing money unnecessarily.

Is There Liquidity Risk?

During durations of high volatility of option and stock bid/ask spreads expand. Regularly play out a worst-case scenario in your head and attempt to determine what the damage might be.

The key is attempting to get a much deeper understanding of the danger related to the position, what option elements affect (time, volatility, stock price motion) it, and how.

Nevertheless, I understand that a few of you have a little bit more danger tolerance than me, so I wished to reveal to you what else to consider when taking on more risk by sizing up.

Don't forget experience is the very best teacher, but I'm likewise here to assist.

Discovering Or Creating Your Own Options Trading System That Works

Stock Options are lovely! This smart derivative of the equities market has to be among the most artistic developments of modern-day times. For the trader who can discover how to win at trading choices, there are many high-ends in life that can be experienced.

Success in options trading needs a consistent approach for long-term success. This declaration is not meant to be grand, idealistic remark made by some 'trading theorist'; instead, it is a declaration born out of the problematic knocks and success experiences of the author and numerous other long-lasting, active trader contemporaries.

This "constant technique" to options trading can also be called a "trading system" or an "option trading system" in this case. The term "trading system" is not always restricted to a series of computerized "black box" trading signals. A trading system might be something as simple as "buy an option on a stock in an uptrend that breaks the high of the previous bar after a minimum of two days of drawback down movement that makes lower lows." A trading system is merely an organized method that benefits from a duplicated pattern or event that brings net revenues.

Considering that an Option is a "Derivative" of the stock, you need to derive your choices trading system from a stock trading system. This indicates your trading system should be based around real stock price movement. That stated, your trading system does not need to work for all stocks. It merely has to work for particular types of stocks, inevitable volatility of stocks and specific cost levels of stocks, etc. Focus your trading system on particular stocks that have cost habits that is predictable to the net results you want to abstract from a stock.

You can design a trading system, a trading method, and a trading approach by determining a price movement pattern (or lack of cost motion pattern) or some occasion that occurs on some sort of routine basis. This means you can trade rate behavior patterns on cost charts such as traditional chart patterns, trends, swings, pivot points, boxes, etc. or you can trade occasions that encourage stock rate such as earnings runs, post revenues runs, stock splits, seasonal aspects, etc.. Bottom line to make the maximum earnings in options trading you desire your stock to relocate your favor quickly, and you want it to move far. A relatively little motion in the rate of a stock can double your money in options!

There are so many various methods and strategies that you can trade with options. You can also enter into ratio back spreads, condors, and butterflies. And if you're feeling insane, you can sell 'naked' options (just better use a stop loss or you'll wind up like among my old trading buddies who ran an account to $20 million then offered everything back offering naked alternatives.)

Directional options trading systems are the very best. Keep it simple, purchase calls for and upside trade or buy puts for a downside trade. But this suggests you need a directional stock trading system to trade directional options.

Here are a couple of various techniques for directional systems:

Establish a choice trading system that trades the swings in stock rate motion. There are lots of excellent swing trading systems available today. We suggest you get one. The bottom line with swing trading is that you wish to swing trade with the trend. Options brokers nowadays have advanced order technology that will allow you to go into swing trades based on the rate movement of the stock, so you do not have to see this stock throughout the day. That significant improvement to swing trading options.

Swing trade the day bars: The majority of swing trading systems are based on daily bars on the stock cost chart.

Swing trade the Intra Day Bars! Their other high systems based on intraday charts that pinpoint swing trading entries.

Establish an options trading system that trades 3 to 6-month trends. This is where the vast money is. Trading the significant patterns is where numerous can place larger amounts of money to develop their net worth.

Develop an options trading system that trades pivot points. Pivot point trading is perhaps the best way to trade choices, since cost action is typically explosive, and occurs rapidly in our instructions when a trade works. Because you can use shorter-term options and take advantage of yourself a little much better, this is good. And it's also excellent you can make fantastic gains in 5 days to 4 weeks typically, so time decay problems end up being less of a worry.

There are various directional trading approaches you could use to trade alternatives. You need to select one, work it, and never use more than 10% options position size per trade on little accounts 1% to 5 % max position size on larger accounts. This exact method of cash management trading options is the fastest method to possibly quick account development, helping you avoid needless setbacks.